MY
SISTER

MY SISTER

How One Sibling's
Transition Changed Us Both

· · · · · · · · · · · · · · · · ·

SELENIS LEYVA
& MARIZOL LEYVA

with Emily Chammah

BOLD TYPE BOOKS

New York

Bold Type Books
116 East 16th Street, 8th Floor New York, NY 10003
www.boldtypebooks.org
@BoldTypeBooks

Printed in the United States of America

First Edition: March 2020

Published by Bold Type Books, an imprint of Perseus Books, LLC, a subsidiary
of Hachette Book Group, Inc. Bold Type Books is a co-publishing venture of
the Type Media Center and Perseus Books.

The Hachette Speakers Bureau provides a wide range of authors for speaking
events. To find out more, go to www.hachettespeakersbureau.com or call
(866) 376-6591.

The publisher is not responsible for websites (or their content) that are not
owned by the publisher.

Print book interior design by Jeff Williams.

Library of Congress Control Number: 2019956080

ISBNs: 978-1-5417-6295-4 (hardcover), 978-1-5417-6296-1 (e-book)

LSC-C

10 9 8 7 6 5 4 3 2 1

To Mami and Papi

CONTENTS

INTRODUCTION

. . . .

I've never had to give much thought to my identity as a woman. I've never had to question who I am or how the world sees me. My body, my mind, my heart—even when I think back to my earliest memories—everything has always felt connected.

From an early age, I played house. I was always the mommy holding the baby doll. When my breasts started to change, I became fully aware that my body was different from those of my brothers and the other boys around me. I always felt somewhat soft and somehow pink. Never did I question my choices in favorite colors or my instant love of Barbies. Never was I made to feel that how I naturally moved, talked, or expressed myself were offensive or wrong. My gender identity was assigned to me at birth and it matched my soul; therefore, it just was—it just *is*—and it has allowed me to just *be*.

But we live in a world in which many of us are constantly told that we can't act a certain way because it isn't "okay."

Some of us must constantly edit our natural movements, expressions, interests to more neatly fit into what is expected of us.

Some of us look into a mirror and the person looking back at us is not the person that lives inside.

1

I have had moments when I've hated my body. Because of weight gain or because my shape didn't match that of most models and actresses. I've wished for fuller breasts, for longer and leaner legs. And I've also had moments when I hated my Afro-Latinx features. As a child, I always felt ugly compared with my cousins, who all had fair skin and nice hair. I remember being stared at or hearing comments that made me look in the mirror and recognize that my features—my skin, my face, my hair—were considered ugly. Every time I looked at my reflection, I wanted to change what I saw. I grew up intensely aware of my flaws, thinking that everyone around me believed that my looks weren't "right."

But it wasn't until my sister Marizol began her transition that I really stopped to think about what she might have been feeling. It wasn't until I saw how desperately she fought to understand herself and what was happening to her that I really took a moment to put myself in her shoes.

I realized only then that I had witnessed Marizol be uncomfortable and isolated for much of her childhood. Marizol off to the side, hesitant. Marizol disappointed with gifts. Marizol in football gear, awkward and bored. Marizol trapped, unable to live her truth. This, of course, was when I knew her not as my sister but as my baby brother, Jose. I remember the first time I tried to understand these memories from her perspective, to understand the emotions that she must have been feeling. Instantly, I was devastated. Only then did I understand that she, like many trans people, had been living in a prisonlike state where something was off. That "something" is superficially seen by the world but deeply felt by the person who is trapped.

The reality is that I would not have given much thought to how it was to be transgender if it hadn't been for my sister. This is not to say I wouldn't have sympathy for the struggle and the injustice people in the trans community face daily but simply that I likely would not have taken the time to fully immerse myself in someone else's experiences, that I would not have been able to comprehend what it truly means to live with a constant disconnect between your heart, body, and soul.

I have been witness to the childhood of a person who, by the age of three, clearly had a disconnect between body and brain. Before her transition, I saw my sister struggle as an awkward little boy, always off in his own world. I saw sadness in moments that should have been filled with happiness. I saw a little boy fight against his natural essence in an attempt to avoid being picked on or scolded. I saw and felt his embarrassment more times than I care to count—and to this day it haunts me.

Though we are living in a more accepting world than we were twenty years ago, my sister still lives in fear. I have been with her when someone "spooks" her in public. That is, when someone calls her out as trans. I have seen the energy of others around us shift when she walks into a room. I have seen the stares.

I have also seen my sister fully celebrated. I have seen her feel beautiful and happy and confident. And I have seen how quickly, with a single look or word, that all can be erased, taken away from her. This is the reason I want to share with you our story. The story of *My Sister*. I hope to have you see, to have you understand and empathize with Marizol's journey. To recognize that she, like all people in the world, deserves to feel safe and be loved. That she deserves to be acknowledged and addressed as the woman she is and always has been.

Marizol and I believe that individuals have the ability to take control of their gender and sexual identities, and that others should respect their choices. We also recognize that the realities of fully realizing oneself, and being properly affirmed by others, can be messy. For over nineteen years, our family and friends knew Marizol by a different gender and name. That knowledge and the habits that formed over years were not easy to revise. Other family members and I would slip, using the wrong pronouns or name.

This is especially complicated when referring to Marizol before her transition.

The story that follows—our story—has been divided into three sections: Part I: Jose, Part II: Beginnings of a Transition, and Part III: Marizol. A short interlude from Marizol comes at the beginning of Part II. The book closes with an epilogue from Marizol and a list of resources that we hope is useful to those seeking help and advice for themselves and friends and family. In the first two sections, I speak freely about my youngest brother, Jose, and use male gender pronouns. This is uncomfortable for me—painful, even—because I know that name and those pronouns to be not just incorrect but also insulting and hurtful. I want to be clear that it is never okay to call out or refer to a trans individual by their birth name. Deadnaming, or "the practice of uttering or publishing the name that a trans person used prior to transition," according to the LGBTQ news and entertainment magazine *The Advocate*, is an act of violence, one that demeans and insults and harms. After a lot of discussion and thought, Marizol and I have decided to be open about the name she was given at birth, but it was a sensitive and highly personal decision, one that not all trans folk would make. It does not give anyone the permission to call her by that name or to call other trans persons by the name or gender they were assigned at birth.

On a similar note: we want to be true to Marizol's experience as she came to discover her gender identity and as she embarked on her journey of transitioning. A major part of these experiences was getting to know others in the LGBTQ+ community, including those at all stages of their transitions. In a few instances, this means describing certain individuals before they began to transition and, thus, by the gender assigned to them at birth, not as the gender they identify with. We've chosen to be clear about this distinction because it was significant for Marizol to see others begin the process of transitioning and to learn that, years later, an individual she once knew also had transitioned. We want to be explicit, however, that we are not deadnaming these individuals but only describing them this way because of how influential they were to Marizol's personal discovery. For the sake of everyone's privacy and personal safety, we have changed the names of these individuals and most others appearing in this book who are outside of our immediate family.

By the end of Part II, the name *Jose* and those incorrect pronouns (*he/him/his*) disappear. From the beginning of Part III, Marizol is presented as Marizol, my sister, and correctly referred to as such. That said, it is important for me to state, and for you, our readers, to understand, that Marizol has always been herself. Though she was assigned male at birth and was known as "Jose" for most of her life, Marizol has always been female. She, however, kept this from our family for quite some time, revealing her true self initially only to the family she was discovering in her LGBTQ+ community. Even after she began to physically transition, Marizol camouflaged and censored herself around relatives. This double life is explored in Part II: Beginnings of a Transition. Marizol was present in the world during this time, but she tried to hide herself away from me and other members of our family. How often I wish, during that time, that I had been more open, more educated, more understanding.

For the most part, our voices are separated by chapter. For some especially high-tension moments, we alternate speaking, back and forth, within the same chapter. In some instances my recollection does not line up perfectly with Marizol's, and we embrace these contradictions. We want to remain true to the reality that memories have funny ways of changing over time, that the details of life experiences and stories are wholly dependent upon the storyteller.

Recently, Marizol and I shared the same thought with one another: As happy as we are that conversations regarding trans rights and representation are more and more common these days, both of us feel, at times, cheated. We feel cheated because, for so many years, we didn't have the language to describe what Marizol was going through. We feel heartbroken that our community—our predominantly low- to middle-class, Black and Brown neighborhood in the Bronx—lacked the kind of openness we see more and more of today, an openness that would have allowed Marizol to thrive at home, in school, and at work. For me, had I had the education and resources I have now, I could have provided a stronger support system. I constantly feel that I failed my sister when she was most in need because I simply didn't know enough. I regret a lot of those early years, when she was at her darkest points and I was so absorbed in my own struggles and pain that I left her to deal with her demons on her own. I cry often thinking back on those times. But I also know that my support has been lifesaving for her. This, unfortunately, isn't always the case. Too many trans and LGBTQ+ youth are without loving, supportive families, and thus are left to fight for their rights—and lives—on their own. Though progress has been made, society at large still has a long way to go in supporting, understanding, and embracing those who feel out of place.

We want to share our experiences—for Marizol, as a trans woman of color, and for myself, as a family member and close ally—to reduce the stigma around transgender individuals. But, ultimately, we are telling our story because we want to offer others—whether they are in the process of transitioning or are watching a loved one transition—hope.

You are not alone, we say. It is a struggle, but it is a struggle both an individual and a family have the power to overcome. We are telling our story so that family and close friends can understand the importance of support. We are telling our story to help our society find empathy for its members who are trans. We are telling our story in the hope that trans people will be not only valued but also celebrated.

Selenis Leyva

Part I

JOSE

· · · · · · · · · · · · · · · · · · ·

Chapter 1

SELENIS

· · · · · · · · · · ·

Whenever I think about Jose as a baby, I think about the crying.

Jose didn't cry like other babies. His cries didn't have that pathetic sweetness, that cuteness that made you want to gobble him up, to swoon and pinch his cheeks. No. His cry was desperate.

From day one, Jose struggled with his existence. From day one, his little body was in turmoil. His mother was an addict, and he spent the first month of his life in the hospital, detoxing. I remember looking down at him in the crib, watching his whole self tremble. He screamed and cried and his little body, furious and desperate, made the entire crib shake. Right away, I knew there was something different about him. And for me, everything changed.

I GREW UP in a traditional immigrant family in the Bronx. My father is from Cuba, and my mother from the Dominican Republic. I am the oldest of their children, and for much of my childhood, I had only two younger brothers: Tony and Tito.

My father is extremely hardworking and resourceful, and throughout his life, he's held many different kinds of jobs; he's worked as a porter, a butcher, a landlord. When I was very young, my father opened his own butcher shop in Harlem. I remember that it was such a point of pride for him: his first business. For me, though, as a young girl, I hated it. It looked like a mini-supermarket with a few groceries for sale, but the meat on display was the main attraction. The smell of the place was unbearably strong, and I found the back room—with pieces of meat hanging from the ceiling, blood splattered everywhere—terrifying. I secretly wished that my dad owned someplace less gross. Still, it was hard to ignore how proud he was of the place, or how important it was to him.

But it was scary at times. The communities in the area were quite segregated (East Harlem, or Spanish Harlem, was predominately Latinx, while Harlem was African American), and tensions were high. My father, though he speaks with a thick accent, is a light-skinned Cuban man who doesn't fit the stereotypes of what Latinx people look like. His shop was in Harlem, in a low-income community near several large housing projects. Many of the people in the community loved my father, and he'd talk about his customers with kindness. Young kids were always coming in, asking him, "Hey, Papi, how are you today?" Older women in the neighborhood playfully flirted with him, giving him hugs and saying, "Looking good today, Papi!" But in addition to stories like these, I remember overhearing other kinds of stories he and my uncles, who worked with him, would tell about the shop. People trying to steal groceries, or how, one night, they were held up at gunpoint. After that incident, my father decided to register for a gun of his own. This terrified me, and my mother as well. She would always stay up late, waiting for my dad to return home. I can remember lying in bed with my eyes open, waiting for the sound of his car pulling into the driveway, telling me that he was safe. Eventually, during another holdup, my father's uncle was shot in the hand, and my father was forced to fire his own gun. No one was seriously injured and no one died that day, thank goodness, but it was enough to get my father thinking about closing the shop for good. After about ten years, he sold it and went on to piece together several jobs to support us—he did construction, drove taxis, worked as a handyman.

My mother, a stay-at-home mom, made extra cash babysitting children from our neighborhood in the Bronx. Growing up, the house was always full of kids. Our home became like a day care, and I, my mother's helper.

Like most firstborn children in immigrant families, I took on a role of authority from a very young age. I'd translate for my parents at the doctor's office, school conferences, any and all appointments a family member might have had. I was expected to read and translate every letter that was delivered to our house. I had to make phone calls, too, and fill out forms, write notes to teachers. Because my parents didn't write or speak English, I had to do everything they could not. And because I was a girl, I was also expected to help my mother babysit.

At first, I loved it. I was playing house! And I got to be the mommy! I changed diapers, heated up bottles. During snack time, I lined the kids up at the table and passed out Cheerios and apple slices. But then there was the flip side: sunny afternoons I'd be stuck inside while my brothers and cousins played out in the *yardita*, their shrieks and laughter creeping through the brick walls of our home. Soon, I began to resent how I had to spend every afternoon indoors taking care of other people's kids. I began to hate translating, and reading letters, and going to parent-teacher conferences and sitting between my mother and my teacher. And then I hated babysitting. I just wanted to be a normal kid.

Mami ran a tight ship. Despite sometimes having up to a dozen children in our home at once, it never felt chaotic. The house was always tidy and always put together, my mother's floors so gleaming you could see your reflection. Like a day care, my mother had a schedule. I remember how, every single day, she looked forward to the serene promise of nap time. And she had rules. Everything child-related was restricted to the back of the house, to the small bedroom that served as the toy room: *el cuarto de los juegos*. There, we set up the Barbie house and train sets and chests of toys. The front half of the house was like a museum. No one was allowed in the living room. The dining room was off-limits. The glass doors were to remain shut. Nothing was to be touched.

WE WERE A typical Latinx family in many ways. And like many Latinx families, our physical characteristics varied widely. Take my brothers and me: we all looked different.

Tony was a really good-looking boy, with beautiful caramel-colored skin like my mother. But thanks to my aunts and uncles, I knew from a young age that he had "*pelo malo*," or bad hair. For their standards, which were culturally inherited, his hair was too kinky. And this, combined with his wild temperament, made him seem unruly all around. Luckily, according to my aunts and uncles, Tony's light eyes were something that "saved" him.

As a child, I secretly favored my youngest brother, Tito, over Tony. Tito was mild-mannered and sweet, the kind of child you want to love and hold and fuss over. I had been conditioned to believe that "good hair" and fair skin were the ultimate signs of beauty, and of the three of us, Tito's skin was the lightest. And he had "*pelo bueno*," these long, soft, beautiful curls that, when no one was looking, I'd brush and tie up with ribbons, like I did with my dolls. With him, I could pretend that I had a baby sister, which is what I always wanted.

I was somewhere in between. My skin tone was lighter than Mami's and Tony's, but darker than Papi's and Tito's. My hair was more *malo* than *bueno*, and my aunts made it a point to always let me know that my hair was a problem. Many of them, at our house for family gatherings every weekend, would comment on the state of my hair before even saying hello to me: "*Ay Dios mio y ese pelo!*" On my dad's side, all of my cousins had *pelo bueno*. And every time we'd play outside or go swimming, and my hair would become kinky, they would make fun of me and tease, "Why does your hair stick out like that?"

Seeing this, my mother tried to help me with my hair. "*No quiero que te vean con este pelo asi,*" she'd say, wanting me to look presentable, and we'd get to work early on Saturday mornings. First, she'd slather my hair in deep conditioner. Then she'd set it in rollers. Next came tugging on my hair so much that my scalp hurt and my head throbbed, all just to get the perfect bun or pig-tails. But then there were weekends when she didn't have time to do my hair, and when my aunts and cousins entered our house, they'd scan my head, making me feel like I was just awful to look at. Eventually, I began to dread these get-togethers, even though I loved playing with my cousins. And if my mother heard them make a comment or crack some kind of joke, I knew that the next weekend I'd be woken up well before Saturday morning cartoons aired to endure another round of hair torture.

I was "*una mulata.*" Latinx cultures, like many cultures around the world, have a history of anti-Blackness that discriminates against those with darker skin and Afro features. Being *mulata* was considered better than being "fully" Black, but only slightly. *Mulatas* are often portrayed as jezebels, the temptresses who get in the way of wholesome relationships. And harmful ideologies like these have been passed down for generations. From a very young age, these awful, racist stereotypes began to haunt me. I always felt different, like an outsider. My aunt, who looked *mulata* herself—but don't tell her that!—would give me "tips" on how to manage and "fix" my hair. But they never worked and always left me feeling even worse.

Today, many individuals vocalize and celebrate an Afro-Latinx identity, and I am proud to embrace it myself. But growing up, it was not a term used in my family or in my community. In many ways, any suggestion of Blackness or African heritage was shunned in my extended family. My parents weren't concerned about who was more Black or who was more white, but those words from my aunts and uncles stung. I became conditioned to believe that light skin and "good" hair were the prerequisites to being attractive. I never felt pretty. Nor was I ever told that I was pretty. And this kind of internalized racism created a deep-seated sense of self-hatred in me, one that brought me years and years of pain. It is something that even today I fight to overcome.

OUR PHYSICAL FEATURES didn't matter to Mami and Papi; they loved us and supported us all the same. And I remember how the dynamic of our home changed when it was just us, our immediate family. This was especially true in the late afternoons, after all of our cousins and the neighborhood kids Mami babysat had left for the day. My brothers and I were expected to clean up our toys before Papi came home from work, but we always had so much energy around this time, amplified by the aroma of dinner that filled the air. We'd run around teasing each other, laughing or fighting while Mami, working hard in the kitchen, called for us to calm down.

But of these warm, cheerful memories, one day sticks out in particular. I was around eight years old, and Tito didn't want to play or run around. He just lay in front of the television, leaving the craziness to Tony and me. Something was off. I saw it in his face and I felt it in the air. I saw it on my mother's face, too; two deep lines—a clear sign that she was worried—formed between her eyes. And I overheard her on the phone with my father talking about Tito. When she hung up, she announced that Papi was coming home early, and this made me even more uneasy.

What I remember next is how Tito sat on the bed wrapped in a blanket with my mother rocking him and holding him close. His skin looked like a ghost's, and though he was only three, heavy, dark circles hung beneath his eyes. My parents were going to take him to the hospital, and when they lifted the blanket from his lap, I saw that his belly was distended, long and taut.

The doctors said that it was non-Hodgkin's lymphoma. Terminal. That my parents should begin making arrangements.

But Mami and Papi refused to give up. They refused to let go of their youngest son without trying everything they possibly could.

Both of my parents are people of deep, sincere faith, though they show it differently—for my mother, it is all about church and prayer, whereas my father is constantly looking for signs. But both have a strong belief in miracles. During the first several weeks of my brother's illness, I didn't see my parents all that often. They spent their time at the hospital by Tito's side. My mother held on to her faith in prayer, but my father needed more guidance and went to see a woman in Brooklyn who read the tarot. She told him that the doctors wanted to operate, but that they shouldn't.

"It isn't the right time," she said.

My father returned to the hospital and told the doctors to wait. They were shocked and tried to insist. But Papi was adamant, too, and instead of major surgery, they performed a biopsy. Later, after receiving the results, the doctors admitted to my parents that surgery likely would have been too much for Tito's frail body to handle and that it could have made his condition worse.

The next time I saw my brother was through a window in the pediatric intensive care unit. He was so thin and his bones so fine, I'm not sure I would have recognized him on my own. He spent three months in the ICU, hooked up to monitors and tubes. During that time, we saw many children come and go. One day, a bed was filled. The next, it was as if no one had ever been there. I was so afraid my brother would one day disappear just like the others.

My parents never wavered in their faith. In a way, those long days in the hospital made their faith even stronger. They prayed and showered my brother with constant love and care. There was not one night that my father spent away from that hospital room; he slept there, in a chair, beside my brother's bed. He and my mother discussed how, if Tito survived, they would help other children in whatever way they could. They didn't know what they meant by this at the time, but they held on tightly to this promise. It was a promise not only to God but also to each other.

Once Tito was out of the hospital, my father took a trip to Puerto Rico. His friend Hector had told him about La Virgen del

Pozo. In 1953, three children saw a young woman floating in a cloud above a natural spring in Sabana Grande. A crown of seven stars circled her head. She wore a white gown, a pale blue cloak, and held a rosary between her hands. When they looked into her eyes, the children were overcome by a deep sense of peace. She continued to appear day after day for over a month, and people from all over the country flocked to the spring. Hector explained to my father that people visit La Virgen from around the world, people who are in search of miracles.

My father packed with him a pair of Tito's pajamas. They were light blue, long pants and a short-sleeved shirt, covered in little yellow tricycles. These pajamas were Tito's favorite, his signature look. In addition to the pajamas, Papi also packed a small pouch of old coins he had collected over the years.

Papi's first stop was a church in Ponce. There, he left the old coins—an offering—to the statue of La Virgen. Next, he traveled to the site in Sabana Grande where La Virgen appeared and a statue of her now stands. He saw the artifacts people in search of miracles had left behind: pictures in frames, toys, wheelchairs, a car. My father kneeled in front of the statue, set down my brother's pajamas, and prayed: "*Si nos concedes la vida de nuestro hijo, si lo salvas de su enfermedad, prometemos ayudar a otros niños.*"

My father returned from his trip, and for the next two years, Tito went through rounds and rounds of chemo and radiation. And then, miraculously, he went into remission. He was cancer free. The doctors didn't know how to explain it. But my parents did. And they were deeply thankful.

My mother had been raised by her eldest sister, whom we called Abuela Mora. She was a small and feisty spiritual woman, a midwife who read tarot cards and used medicinal teas concocted from the herbs in her garden to heal all who came to her. She was always smiling—and a loving mischief danced in her eyes. My mother loved and respected her deeply, and so when she said that Mami and Tito should go to Higüey to pay homage to La Virgen de Altagracia, the patron saint of the Dominican Republic, the

16

two of them went. They visited the Basílica Catedral Nuestra Señora de la Altagracia, one of the most sacred spaces for many Dominicans, and my mother gave thanks for my brother's life.

Papi had his own way of saying thanks: One day he brought home with him a statue he had purchased at a shop in the South Bronx. It was of La Virgen de la Caridad, the patroness of Cuba. She wears a blue and gold robe beneath a tall crown and holds the child Christ in her arms. She is held up by angels, who hover above a small boat with three men, lost in a rough sea, looking up at her in wonder. Every morning, my father greets the statue. He touches her and thanks her for saving his son's life. When he returns home, he presents her with yellow roses on the stem.

My parents did not forget their promise to help other children. After she returned from the Dominican Republic, my mother began sending boxes and boxes of children's clothing to her village for those in need. She continues to do so to this day. My father, likewise, has donated to Saint Jude's research fund for years. But once Tito was healthy and in kindergarten, they thought of another way they could keep their promise.

EL CUARTO DE *los juegos* in the back part of our house was the first thing to change. Suddenly, the toys were out and in came a crib, a little set of drawers, a bed. My brothers and I were disappointed that our playroom was gone.

"Why do we need any more kids?" Tony asked.

But I knew what it meant: soon, we would have babies in the house. Maybe I could finally have a little sister of my own.

"Can't we ask for just girls?" I asked Mami.

"*Eso no es asi, Mima,*" she said, shaking her head. It didn't work that way.

Enter into our lives a cast of babies from the direst of situations. Babies who had been neglected and abused. Kids with anger issues or behavioral problems. One had cigarette burns along his arms.

Another was HIV-positive. Most didn't stay with us for long, and it was always difficult to say goodbye. But Mami always reminded me: "*Estos niños se quedarán con nosotros hasta que sus padres se mejoren.*" The ultimate goal was, always, for children and their parents to end up together once the parents got better.

It was about a year into our journey as a foster family when Jose came into our lives. We were told that his mother did not hold Jose after he was born. And she couldn't nurse him, of course, on account of the drugs. Jose never had that comforting feeling of his mother's skin on his skin, and that broke my heart. Even though I was young, just a teenager, from day one I went out of my way to give Jose extra attention and care. I wanted to make sure that he knew love. I'd give him baths, putting powder and beautiful-smelling soaps and lotions all over him. Now, as a mother myself, I have an even more profound sympathy for this baby, born into the world without his mother there to hold him, uncomfortable in his own body, fighting for his life. But at the time, I thought, *This baby doesn't have a mommy.* As a little girl, I loved playing mommy with my dolls—and now I could do it with a real baby.

I became obsessed with Jose. My mother was devoted to him, too, of course, but I was attached to him in a way I hadn't been with the others. I knew that, as a foster baby, Jose might not be in our lives forever. At any moment, he could be returned to his birth parents or sent to a different home. But that didn't stop me. I spent all of my time with Jose. He was mine. My chunky little baby doll. And he became attached to me, too. Whenever I went to school or to a friend's house or even just down the block, I had to leave him with a shirt or a piece of clothing that smelled like me so that he could sleep. Very quickly, he became a happy, chubby baby. He became part of our family. And I was protective of him.

Jose's father was in prison, but every week his mother was scheduled to appear at the agency for visitation. Ruth was a very pretty woman with curly black hair and a swipe of bright red lipstick. I didn't want to like her—and not simply because of what she'd done to Jose. I didn't want to like her because she was a threat. It would be her who took Jose, this baby I loved so deeply, away from us. My mother didn't see her this way. Instead, she saw a woman who was struggling, a woman who needed help. Mami was always kind to Ruth. Friendly, even. I was not. I hated the way she always seemed jumpy. I hated the way she was constantly sweaty. (Signs, of course, that she once again was using, though I didn't know this at the time.) I hated the way she tried to be affectionate with Jose, kissing and hugging him. I hated how she'd comment on how cute he was dressed or how nice he smelled. I hated that when he came home from these visits, his clothes would smell like her perfume and his face would be covered in red lipstick.

Looking back, I think that she was embarrassed. She didn't have a connection to this baby; because she was high for most of her pregnancy, I don't think she allowed for that kind of connection to develop. And these grand shows of affection seemed to be a way for her to compensate for what wasn't there. On top of this, I think Ruth knew that I was protective of Jose (and I doubt I did a great job of hiding my feelings toward her), and I'm sure that made her uneasy, or even more embarrassed. She'd often say to me, "He's like your little doll!"

Yeah, I'd think. MY *doll.*

Over time, Jose became less and less tolerant of Ruth's affection. It was clear that a bond was forming with us, the ones who cared for him, and whenever she tried to hold him, he'd pull away. If I was in the room with them, he was inconsolable until he was back in my arms, safe. It didn't help that, as time passed, her visits became infrequent. She started missing appointments, sometimes for weeks in a row.

In response to this rejection from her own baby, Ruth turned angry and cold. This made Jose want to be around her even less. After a few visits, my mother told me to stop coming. It would be easier for all of us, she said, Jose included, if I wasn't there.

"*Cuando tu estas el no quiere estar con Ella,*" she said, indicating that she knew Jose preferred me to Ruth but that Ruth deserved a chance with her own baby.

Fine with me, I thought. I didn't want to see that woman anyways. It was hard for me to pretend to like her.

Ruth became more inconsistent with her visits. After several months of no-shows, my parents began the process of legally adopting Jose, who was becoming more and more integral to our family unit. But whenever they got close to finalizing the adoption, Ruth would reappear, wanting to see her son. Emotionally overwhelmed and distraught, my mother couldn't imagine caring for another infant at this time. She called the agency and told them that we could no longer take any more children.

LATE ONE NIGHT in the early nineties, the phone rang. I was already in bed but curious. I walked down the long hallway from my bedroom to the small dining room, where the house phone sat on a little table.

"Hello?"

It was Ms. Hernandez, the social worker. I knew her well because of all the children who had come through our house. She was always friendly and kind. That night, she asked to speak to my mother.

"But she's asleep," I said.

"It's an emergency."

I crept back down the hall to my parents' room to wake up my mother. There was a phone in their room, but she didn't take the call there so as not to wake my father. I walked with her back to the dining room and listened as she spoke.

"Oh, *una nina*," Mami said.

It was a girl! I started waving my arms, motioning to her: *Please say yes!* But even then, I saw the exhaustion on her face.

"*Lo siento,*" she said into the handset, her eyes on me, "*pero no puedo en este momento.*"

She hung up the phone, and the two of us stood there, looking at one another.

"Mami, it's a little girl, a baby!" I wanted a little sister so badly. "Why did you say no?"

"*Es que no puedo mas,*" she said. She was tired, and everything that had been going on with Jose was just too much.

"I know, Mami. But the baby girl needs someone. I'll help you, I promise." I knew I was laying it on thick.

"Okay," she said finally and called Ms. Hernandez back. I stood right next to her, my ear to the phone so that I could hear.

"Oh, well thank you," Ms. Hernandez said, "we've already placed her. But we just got a call about another little girl—are you willing to take her?"

"Yes, of course. We'll take her."

It took several hours for the agency to process everything and get the baby to us. We didn't know anything other than she was removed from her mother and that she was nine months old. Isalyn arrived well after midnight, a lanky, beautiful baby girl. She didn't have anything but the clothes she was wearing, but she was curious, with big round brown eyes that looked directly into mine. She grabbed at my hair and didn't cry once. Later, in my bed, I was so excited, I couldn't sleep. I was so happy to finally have a baby sister.

THE ADDITION OF Isa to our home meant that we had two babies to care for. And for a while, everything seemed to be okay. Isa and Jose were bonding with us and one another, and we all felt so lucky to have these beautiful babies in our lives. But then, things took a turn. After disappearing for several months yet again, Ruth suddenly reappeared with Jose's birth father. Jose Sr. was finally out of prison, and they were trying to be a family. With a baby girl on the way, even.

Mami invited them over to our home for a visit. This was not a common thing to do. Typically, all visits were organized exclusively through the agency. But because of my mother's trust, kindness, and love for baby Jose, she gave them more access. Now, I recognize that she did this as a way to maintain a connection with them and thus protect Jose. She knew how the system worked. She knew that the agency had a reputation for turning over children to their biological parents well before they needed to. And in many ways, her friendliness toward this couple worked: when Jose was baptized, Ruth and Jose Sr. asked Mami to be his godmother.

I, however, did not have as much patience. Right away, from the moment he walked into our house, I didn't like Jose Sr. He was full of machismo, claiming his territory and making his presence known. He was also overly friendly—but not in a sincere way. He was making a show. He smiled too much and spoke too loud. He was jumpy. I didn't trust him.

We all sat awkwardly in the living room. The floors were shining, and fresh yellow roses adorned my father's statue of La Virgen de la Caridad.

"Come and kiss me," Jose Sr. said to the baby. "I'm your father! Call me Papi."

Jose turned his head, tried to pull away.

Ruth, looking full and healthy in her pregnancy, seemed embarrassed by the rejection. "It's okay," she said. "Just let him be."

"No, I'm his father. Papi! Come say hello to your father." Jose Sr. pulled baby Jose close to him, held him so that he couldn't go.

Jose screamed. He didn't know them. He didn't want to be hugged or kissed or touched by them. *We are his family!* I thought. *Not you!* Tears streamed down Jose's cheeks. But Jose Sr. insisted.

"I'm your father!"

Always kind, my mother tried to talk him down. "*Compai*, you have to calm down. He's scared."

"But I just love my son!" Jose Sr. cried, finally letting little Jose go. "I just want my son to love us!"

"I know, *Compai*. I know."

When it was time for them to go, Ruth didn't force Jose to come say goodbye. She kissed and hugged my mother and then, holding on to her pregnant belly, said, "He's happy with you."

After their second child was born, Ruth and Jose Sr. began to have Jose stay with them for unsupervised overnight visits. This made us all nervous. We knew it wasn't a good idea, and none of us could understand why, after years of Ruth failing drug tests and disappearing for months at a time, the system suddenly trusted her to care for a child she didn't know. It was clear to us that the agency wasn't aware Jose Sr. was living with Ruth, that they were not following up with visitations or inquiries. Thinking back, I question how it was possible that they could just forget about Jose and not monitor the situation with his birth mother at all. Over the years, I've heard too many horror stories about children in the foster care system who suffered. I wonder often about the many others who also fell through the cracks.

Whenever a visit was coming up, and my mother mentioned it to my father, I'd object and get angry. And Mami would turn to me, looking defeated, and say, "*Yo no puedo decirle que no.*" The court had made its decision, and we had to follow it.

And then, after we had cared for Jose for three years, the system returned him to his biological family. He was just a toddler. I hated that he was gone, that he was no longer part of our family. My mother hated it, too, but she had done what she had promised: she had cared for Jose while Ruth and Jose Sr. got themselves together, and now they had the chance to be a family.

For a few weeks we heard nothing from Ruth or Jose Sr., but about a month had passed when Ruth's mother called my mother.

"You have to come get him," she said, her voice shaking, out of breath. "You have to come get him because this isn't good for him."

"He's crying all the time," she said. "He's sad."

And so my mother and father went. When they got him home, my mother and I gave Jose a bath, just like we had always done.

He was angry and crying, splashing the water out of the tub. And out of nowhere, Jose slapped Mami across the face.

Some of the children we had stay with us had behavioral problems. Some of them were angry and would lash out physically. Throw things. Scream or hit. But not Jose. He had always been a happy baby. A sweet, loving, affectionate baby. This was something new.

Mami stopped washing and pulled Jose against her chest, rocking him back and forth while he cried.

"It's okay, baby," she said. "It's okay. You will never leave here."

Later, my mother noticed a bruise on Jose's calf, just behind the knee, that bore a distinct resemblance to the mark a belt would leave.

"Who did this to you?" she asked.

Jose looked at her for a moment, his eyes wide and full of fear. Finally, he said, "Jose."

Immediately, Mami called Jose Sr. "I saw the bruise," she said. "Just know that this isn't going to happen again because if it does, I am calling the police."

"Oh, how could you say that, Comay? I love him—he's my son!"

"I'm just letting you know," she said, and hung up the phone.

She was doing all that she could to protect Jose, and I wanted to do the same.

Chapter 2

SELENIS

. . . .

In our family—like in most other Latinx families—the sense of machismo was prevalent. Gender roles were rigid, defined. Growing up, hardly ever did I see my father wash a dish or help tidy up the house or wash clothes or even watch us when my mother had to step out. Papi would often be heard saying things like, "*Eso es cosa de mujeres,*" or "Men don't do that!" And the only time anyone mentioned the words *gay* or *homosexual* was as the butt of a joke. At family gatherings, my father and his brothers would laugh and make fun of their cousin's gay son. Even though I was young, a pit hardened in my stomach. *That isn't nice,* I thought.

In his early years, Jose didn't speak or babble like other babies. If he couldn't reach something—a fork, a toy, a crayon—he'd extend his arm, point his finger, and grunt. We tried to get him to use words, to have him ask for what he wanted, but my mother knew he needed more help. She discussed the situation with his caseworker, and Jose was evaluated. Because of his birth mother's drug use while pregnant, he had developmental issues and was placed in a school in northwest Manhattan that specialized in speech therapy. He was three years old when he first spoke, and right away, his personality came through in a way it never had before. And as he grew, I began to notice his movements, how he didn't encounter the world the way my brothers or other little boys did. Here was Jose with tightly cropped hair, dressed in little boys' clothes, walking around, hands on his hips, *tsssking*—like a sassy little girl. I thought to myself, *Well, this is what it is. Everyone better learn how to deal.*

My mother noticed it, too. And though we never verbalized it, there was a moment when we looked at each other, almost to say, *How do we feel about this? We're fine.* But we knew, from then on, that we had to be the ones to take charge and protect Jose. We had to protect him from my father, from my brothers, from anyone else in our family. We had to protect him from the jokes, from that constant question: *Why can't you be more like a man?*

IN EIGHTH GRADE, I was accepted to LaGuardia High School for the Performing Arts. It was the school I had dreamt of attending ever since I saw the TV show *Fame*. The way the students danced on tables, sang out loud in the hallways, took acting classes— these were things I wanted to experience. My middle school guidance counselor told me early on that getting into a school like that for a girl like me—a girl from the Bronx with no acting experience—would be impossible. He gave me instead a short list of schools that had good secretarial programs, but I knew I had to go to LaGuardia. I begged him for the application, which he literally threw at me. He stopped me as I left his office with the application in hand.

"Remember what I told you," he said, "when you don't get in."

I went straight to the library. The application said that I needed two monologues for the audition. My first thought was, *Okay, I need to know what a monologue is.* I researched and researched, and finally chose two. One was from *Rashomon*, and not appropriate at all for a fourteen-year-old, but I was very dramatic, and thought I could use it to show off my skills. I practiced my pieces over and over, watching myself in my bedroom mirror.

On the day of the audition, I was so nervous. I made my mother take the train with me to Manhattan. The audition went great! It was the callback that didn't go well. About halfway through, I began to notice all of the people in the room, and I blanked on my lines. I regrouped and pushed through to the end.

The next few weeks of waiting were painful. But then, my acceptance letter arrived. I was so happy and excited, and my family was so proud. This was a huge opportunity for me, the child of immigrants who spoke little English. That fall, while all of my friends stayed in the Bronx and went to the local high school, I ventured out into "the city." But attending LaGuardia was overwhelming. For the first time in my life, I was out of the Bronx, out of my comfort zone. For the first time in my life, I was one of just a few Latinxs. Suddenly, everything about me was different, strange. The fact that I spoke with an accent. That I was from anywhere other than Manhattan. That I hadn't gone to private school or taken acting classes with Big Name Professionals. That my hips weren't narrow, slim. I listened to different music and didn't know the movies everyone talked about. My classmates made it clear that I wasn't like them, and they teased me in the simplest of ways. I had a long leather jacket that I'd gotten from a store on Fordham Road. I remember the smell of leather, how the girls from my neighborhood stared at me with envy when I walked up to them in my new jacket. They loved it, and so did I. But at LaGuardia, no one complimented me. Every morning, some girl would look me up and down and say, "Who wears that?"

I felt alone, like I had no one. Every day, I took the train by myself from 205th Street in the Bronx, transferred to the 1 Train, and got off at West 66th Street–Lincoln Center. It was an hour each way. And every day, I came home worn down and exhausted, feeling defeated. At home, I cried myself to sleep. At school, I excused myself from class to cry in the bathroom. I hated LaGuardia. I barely made any friends. My classmates made me feel dumb, ugly, and untalented. I missed my old friends. I missed laughing at the familiar jokes. The kids at LaGuardia acted so cool. They smoked and drank. They talked about how much they hated their parents, how they were in therapy, or how many times they had tried to kill themselves. It felt like a game, like everyone was trying to one-up one another to become the tortured-artist type. Granted, not everyone was like this, and some students were really suffering. Eventually, I found a handful of kids that made my life at LaGuardia a little less painful, a little less lonely.

AT HOME, THOUGH, I had Jose. And, even for just short amounts of time, he made me forget all that I was going through. When I opened the front door, Jose whooped and cheered. "Seli's home! Seli's here!" He danced around the room, chanting my name: "Sel-li! Sel-li!" Every day was a parade. Every day, a celebration.

"All right, all right," I'd say. "Yes, I'm home!"

But Jose couldn't contain himself. He would hold on to my wrists and jump up and down.

I'd grab a snack and sit down in front of the TV. Then, Jose would begin our ritual.

My other brothers—Tito and Tony—never wanted to do my hair. Isa, my youngest sister, wasn't all that interested either. Every so often she'd want to give me a ponytail, but when she did it was awful. She'd yank the brush through my hair. She jerked my head around so it was in the right place for her, completely oblivious as to how uncomfortable it was for me. The ponytail would be crooked, the hair pulled tight against my scalp, but lumpy.

Jose, however, was always soft. I remember how he would watch me, how he'd follow me around the house, mimicking my movements and expressions. I recognized this as a sign of his attachment and love. But now, I see that I was the symbol of what he really wanted to be, or an example of how he saw himself.

At first, it started out with just his fingers massaging my scalp, breaking up knots and snags like combs. His little hands were always gentle, so soothing. Then, one day, he added a brush. Quickly, our ritual became more elaborate, with styling products, clips, and pins. Later, he graduated from hair to makeup, putting lipstick and eyeshadow on me. When I sat down in Papi's recliner in my parents' bedroom to watch TV, Jose rushed to the half-bathroom where my mother kept her makeup and supplies to grab the basket of brushes and hairsprays. He climbed up on the chair to stand behind me, his feet pressing into the cushion, his legs and hips leaning into the chair's back. For me, it was so relaxing, like getting a massage. It was perfect.

But we weren't supposed to be doing this. Papi didn't like it, and he told me explicitly that what Jose was doing wasn't for boys. Even Mami, who was kind and accepting, warned us. "*Ya tu papa te lo advirtió*," she'd say, not wanting problems when Papi came home. Isa threatened to tell on us sometimes, and my brothers, who often brought home friends, would make sly comments. "Doing hair again?" they'd ask. Whenever they were around, I watched Jose shrink into the chair. He lost his confidence. He lost the excitement and joy he had when it was just the two of us.

Sometimes, even after such harsh reminders, Jose and I would be sitting on the couch, surfing through midafternoon talk shows or cartoons, and out of nowhere, it seemed, a brush would appear. I felt Jose scoot closer to me, reach out, and stroke my head. Soon, he was behind me, the brush in his hand, parting and smoothing my hair. He was calm and happy; comfortable, even. In these moments, Jose was able to be himself. And I would be able to relax after my long, lonely day. I needed the comfort of what felt safe and familiar. The soothing touch on my head would even make me sleepy, and we both got lost in those moments. That is, until we heard the soft clap of a car door in the driveway or, if we were really into it, the jingle of Papi's keys at the side door. Then Jose was outta there, leaving the products and styling tools on the floor. Pretending like he'd never been there at all. It's funny to think about how we hid something so innocent, so harmless, from everyone else. But Jose's fear of being caught was real, and I never wanted him to get in trouble.

AFTER JOSE CAME back to us with the bruise on his leg, Mami refused to let him go to overnight or unsupervised visitations with his birth parents, despite what the courts or the agency had ordered. The visits from Ruth and Jose Sr. to our home became infrequent, but the phone calls from Jose Sr. were constant.

Every time the phone rang, Jose would look at the caller ID. If he saw it was his father, he'd barely lift the phone off of the receiver before setting it back down and hanging up. And I did the same. Some days, if the phone kept ringing and ringing and ringing, I'd turn the answering machine off and silence the ringer. It'd be this way for a while, and I'd even forget—until Mami went to check the messages. She'd look confused and ask us, "*Que le paso al telefono?*"

I would feign ignorance. "*No sé!*"

I didn't want to talk to Jose Sr., and I knew that Jose didn't want to either. I just didn't quite know why.

DANCE CLASSES WERE a substantial part of my high school education. I loved performing and being onstage, but when I stood in front of the ceiling-to-floor studio mirrors with the rest of the girls in my class, all of those parts of my body I felt self-conscious about suddenly seemed amplified. Most of the girls were so thin. I had thick legs, wide hips, and a round butt. I tried to diet so that I could be more like everyone else—but I began to obsess. And very quickly, it turned into something much worse.

At first, I made myself throw up. Then, I just stopped eating altogether. In the mornings, I bought tea from the bodega and slowly sipped the tepid liquid throughout the day. At home, I'd move food around on my plate so it looked like I was eating something. But then I took it to the kitchen and threw it away. I got thinner and thinner, and the girls in my class praised me.

"Oh my God! You're so skinny!"

One day at school, I felt really dizzy. The room started to spin, and I nearly fainted.

The school nurse questioned me. "Did you eat today?"

By this point, I was an expert at covering for myself.

"Oh, it's not that," I said. "I think I'm coming down with the flu."

At home, my mother expressed her concern at how thin I'd become. "*Estas muy flaca!*" she said. "*Tienes que alimentarte, tienes que comer!*"

My hair started to fall out, too. I was clearly not healthy. But I just shrugged, said, "I eat ... it's just all the dance classes."

Mami had so much going on—raising five children and juggling the demands of Jose's situation with his parents—that she didn't have time to question it. And so she wrote it off as part of this acting world she didn't understand. I was the eldest, the one who was going places. The one who was getting praise from her teachers.

Or, from one teacher in particular.

My math teacher my first year at LaGuardia was overly attentive. I hated his class. Not only because I have always struggled with math but because he creeped me out. He would start sweating profusely when he stood way too close to me. He would hover over my desk in a way that felt like he was invading my space.

"You seem really tired," he said. "I could give you some vitamins to help you."

"Um, no thanks," I said, leaning away from him. *Oh my God, please don't sweat on me!* "I'm fine."

At night, he called me at home. My parents did not find this strange at all. For them, people who are doctors, police, teachers are authority figures who are to be respected; they know all. And for a teacher to call me, at home, after hours—well, it seemed like something to be proud of. "Oh, she's getting a call from her teacher! She must really be liked."

I didn't know how to tell them that he was freaking me out. That his calls to me at night before I went to bed felt wrong. That they were wrong. He spoke in a whispery voice, offering to help me with math after school. He tried to get me to open up to him about what was "wrong" with me, to tell him why I seemed lost or disinterested in his class. Every chance he got, he tried to offer me "vitamins." As he stood behind me in class, I could feel the heat from his body and the way he looked at me, and it was more than I could take. He made me feel uncomfortable and self-conscious, but I questioned my feelings. He never physically touched me or harmed me, and a part of me questioned whether it was enough just to say that he made me uncomfortable. I felt like no one would believe me, and I didn't want to make any problems for myself at this school I'd dreamed of attending. But, eventually, I felt like I had to say something to someone, and I decided to tell the guidance counselor. He was very surprised when I told him, and he took me to one of the deans' offices. The two of them spoke in private for a few minutes, and then I was asked to sit and share the details with my dean.

I remember the way he looked at me; it was a look of anger. *Why was he angry with me?* He asked to speak to me in private, and as the guidance counselor was leaving, the dean said, "Don't close the door—we don't want her to accuse *me* of anything."

Now it was just the two of us, the dean sitting behind his desk, telling me that I was exaggerating and needed to stop being silly. I never went back to that math class or the guidance counselor again. And when one of our acting teachers commented on my body and asked whether I was sexually active and tried to hold my hand, I knew I had to handle it myself. I made sure to never be alone with him. And as I got older and more confident, I was able to handle his advances like most of the other girls in the department did: I'd laugh him off or say something sassy or roll my eyes. This made him laugh and, thankfully, he'd let the topic go.

Thinking back on these moments angers me. It angers me that interactions like these are common experiences for women. I wish that I would have had the support to speak out, that I had been believed instead of treated like I was a threat. It is also clear to me now that, because I came from a working-class background, because my parents were not involved in school activities, because I came from a family of immigrants who didn't speak English, because I was a young woman of color, I was, in many ways, a perfect target. Now, as a mother of a young woman, I am happy that the #MeToo movement has given voice to those who have otherwise been silenced like I once was. I can only hope that this kind of support will continue and that bad behavior by men in power, whether in Hollywood or in the education system, will no longer be tolerated.

WHEN JOSE WAS eight, Jose Sr. went back to prison in New York City, and soon after he was deported to the DR. Then Ruth fell back into drugs hard, and her daughter Yvette came to live with us. By then my mother was no longer working with the agency but was asked to house Yvette not only because of her experience as a foster parent but also because of the bond between Yvette and Jose.

Jose and Yvette were so similar, in both personality and looks. I remember the two of them sitting next to one another, playing nicely and sharing, marveling at how the color of their skin, the shape of their eyebrows, their smiles, their teeth—even their toes!—were the same. The two of them had a connection, a friendship Jose didn't share with our sister Isa. Jose and Isa were constantly at it; 98 percent of the time that they played together, they ended up fighting. But with Yvette, he seemed at ease. Perhaps it was their unspoken bond or simply the novelty of having her around, a sister all of his own.

Six children in one home, however, is a lot. And in terms of finances and space, it was impossible for my parents to keep up. My mother wanted to make sure that Yvette was safe, that she had someone to care for her. But she also knew that we couldn't keep her forever. Mami told Ruth that she would keep her for a time, on the condition that Ruth got herself together.

But Ruth couldn't. We knew something was very wrong when she failed to show up for visitations with the seven-year-old daughter she had always wanted and cared for and loved since birth.

Mami was disappointed. But we were tapped out. And so the system took Yvette away and placed her in another home.

While Yvette was still living with us, a friend of mine from LaGuardia told me about a kids production of *The Lion King* she was putting together. I immediately thought of Jose, how he'd beg to help me practice my lines, to learn whatever dance moves I was rehearsing, to wait for me to count "and a five-six-seven-eight!" *This will be perfect*, I thought, and I signed up all three of the little ones—Jose, Isa, and Yvette. Isa never really expressed much interest in performing or in anything artistic, but I wanted them to all do something together. And so every weekend, I took them into the city, to the rehearsal space in Harlem. At home, we rehearsed their lines. Isa and Jose argued because Jose would say Isa's lines and do all of her parts. He really seemed to enjoy every moment of it.

The performance was adorable, of course. Of all of them, the one who really shined was Isa. There was a moment when she got a huge laugh from the audience. Her little face lit up and she really owned the part. I was pleasantly surprised! But with Jose—I watched him lurk in the back awkwardly. It was the opposite of how he acted at home during our private rehearsals. I watched him shrink like he did when Tito's and Tony's friends teased him about doing my hair. Theater requires an openness, a freedom that I thought would allow Jose's true self to shine. But instead of filling the room with his energy, I watched him be a shy little boy, embarrassed by the dozens of faces staring up at him, watching his every move.

Chapter 3

MARIZOL

. . . .

Of all of my siblings, Seli was my favorite. I wanted to be near her all the time. When she was at school, I spent the whole day waiting. And if the phone rang, I asked Mami right away: "Is it Seli? Where is she? Is she coming home?"

I would always sneak into her room, play with her makeup and clothes. I made tube tops out of her scarves and shirts. I wanted to feel what it was like to have long hair like she had, and so I pulled the neck of a T-shirt up onto my head, just over my ears, and let it fall down my back. But it was too loose and kept slipping off. I tried the sleeve of the shirt instead, and it was just the right size. It stayed snug around my forehead as I moved around Seli's room, looking into her mirror and touching her pretty clothes. I loved feeling the weight of the fabric swing as I walked.

When she was finally at home, Seli let me do her hair. She sat on the couch, or in Papi's big chair, and I ran to *el baño chiquito* to grab the products, the combs, the brushes and pins. I piled them in the small basket Mami kept under the sink and raced back to Seli, chanting to myself, *Yes, yes, yes, yes!* Climbing on the cushions behind her, I laid out my supplies in a line and pulled the brush through her dark brown hair. With her, I could experiment with new styles—a ponytail, pigtails, a braid. When I was a little older, she let me put lipstick on her lips or shiny polish on her nails.

Sometimes, Isa would walk in and catch us.

"He's not supposed to be doing that!" she would say. "I'm going to tell Papi."

Papi would be mad if he knew. He told me I wasn't allowed to do Seli's hair, that this kind of thing wasn't for boys. I was afraid of getting in trouble, that Isa would tell him.

But Seli always stood up for me. "No, you're not," she'd say.

And Isa would slink away, embarrassed and afraid of our older sister, and for a few moments, before I heard Papi's car in the driveway or the clank of the gate at the far end of the *yardita* or the jingle of his many, many keys, before I ran to return the basket and products to their place, I felt free, comfortable, happy. I felt like me.

At that age, I watched my brothers and sisters each doing their own thing, each having their own outlet to express themselves—Isa had her Barbies, my brothers, basketball, and Seli, acting. When I wasn't doing Seli's hair or nails, I felt sad and lost. Like a kid who didn't know who she was. I wished that I didn't have to put it all away when my dad came home, that my brothers didn't make fun of me for liking these "girly" things. I wished that I could have been open and confident about who I was because, whenever it was time to hide it, time to pretend to be someone I wasn't, I fell into a dark, lonely place. I was grateful for those few moments I had with Seli; they were my favorite moments of the day. I just wished it could have been like that all the time.

THE HOLIDAYS were big in our house. Birthdays, anniversaries, Christmas, family get-togethers—Mami and Papi hosted all the parties and celebrations. I always looked forward to that time of year when it was time for Seli and Isa and me to deck out the front of the house with decorations. I especially liked Halloween, because it was my job to pass out the candy.

Hosting all the parties meant that we always had so much food in our house. *Arroz con gandules. Pernil.* Potato and macaroni salads.

In the summers, Papi would buy a whole pig to roast, and he and Tito and Tony and the rest of the men would gather in the driveway, watching the pig brown in the pit Papi had made himself. During the fall, I watched Mami prepare the *pasteles* in the kitchen: how she'd grate the *platanos* to make a masa, adding a little achiote oil for flavor; how she'd combine the chicken or *pernil* with the doughy mixture before wrapping it in a banana leaf and parchment and stringing it up. Mami would make so many, we would have enough to last us from Thanksgiving till New Year's. By the time everyone else arrived, all done up in fancy clothes, Mami would still be working in the kitchen with rollers in her hair.

As soon as the guests entered our home, it seemed, the men and women separated: the women would gather in the kitchen and gossip, and the men would drink and play dominoes or sit in front of the TV to watch the big game. I liked being with Mami and the other ladies, but even there, I felt a little strange, a little bit out of place. Like I was some kind of outcast, somehow different from everyone else. My aunt would often say to me, "Why are you always with the women? Why don't you go out there and be with the men?" Reluctantly, I'd leave the room to go be with Papi, with my brothers and cousins and uncles. I never felt like I belonged there or like I could relate to them. For one thing, everyone was older than me. But there was something deeper telling me that I didn't fit in I hovered on the edge of the room, listening to them talk about "guy stuff" or watching them watch football, wishing I could feel at ease. I'd drift back to where the ladies were and try not to attract too much attention—I didn't want my aunt to call me out again.

It was hard always being kind of in between, and I tried to hide these feelings. I wanted to join in the laughter and celebration that was all around me, but sometimes it was difficult, even as a little kid, to get out of my head and be in the moment. Everyone was always happy, having a good time. And I was happy to be around my family, but I didn't feel like I could be myself. I didn't even know what it meant for me to be myself, because everyone was always telling me that I was in the wrong place or liking the wrong things.

One thing I loved about the parties was all the dancing. No one ever taught me how to dance, but I learned through watching everyone salsa and merengue around the house. I looked forward to that point in the evening when, after the adults had sipped on their rum and coquito, Papi would start singing old-school ballads and mariachi songs. (Even though Papi is Cuban, he loves mariachi music.) He'd pull Mami into the middle of the living room, where the two of them danced, swaying back and forth in the glow of the Christmas tree. I watched them, the beat of the music in my chest, wanting to join in but feeling shy. And then, without saying anything, someone would grab my hand and pull me onto the dance floor. It was Seli, of course, and she and I would dance with Isa and the rest of our cousins and aunts and uncles until late in the night.

OTHER PEOPLE in my life I knew were my "family": my biological mom and dad—Ruth and Jose Sr. were their names—and my sister, Yvette, who lived with them. I liked playing with Yvette. Mami and Papi would invite her over, and she and Isa and the neighborhood kids and I all played together in the *yardita*. We'd jump rope, play monkey-in-the-middle and catch. Mami didn't want us running out into the street, so if the ball went over the fence, we had to shout for someone to come outside and bring it to us. But sometimes, if we were feeling especially bold, we'd open the gate and run to grab the ball before it rolled from the sidewalk into the street, crouching low so that no one could see.

When I was very little, Mami took me into the city every weekend to see Ruth. I hated going. I hated riding the D train for over an hour to sit in the dark, stale lobby, not knowing if she would show up or not. When she did show up, she was always nervous and jittery. Like she couldn't ever sit still. And in her eyes it always seemed like she was somewhere off in the distance, very far away. I remember that she was always kind to me, always quick to tell me: "Oh, my baby, I love you. I love you. I love you." She kissed me all over, leaving bright red lipstick marks all over my face. When it was time to go, I watched a sadness take over her face. And somehow I felt that she was sad because she couldn't be with me.

Later, Jose Sr. came to these meetings.

"*Bendicion,* Papi."

He said this to me every time I saw him and every time he called our house. He wanted it to be a special greeting between us. He wanted me to nod and repeat it to him: "*Bendicion,* Papi." But I did not want to talk to him at all.

And then, one day, I found myself living with my biological family. Ruth wasn't around—it was just Yvette and me and Jose Sr. and Miguel, Ruth's teenage son. I didn't like living there, even though I was with Yvette. I missed Mami and Papi and Seli—and Tito and Tony and Isa, too. I missed the warmth of our home. I missed the way the hardwood floors shined, how Mami's collection of little angel statues were delicately arranged in the formal living room, the fresh flowers that were everywhere. I missed the way Papi'd come home on Friday night, with a bouquet for Mami in one hand and a large pizza from the shop nearby his work that he knew she loved in the other. I missed the light and laughter and love.

Ruth and Jose Sr.'s house was dark. My memory of the time I stayed there is foggy, but certain images come to mind: the floor covered in cheap, imitation-wood tiles that peeled around the edges; a TV that sat on top of an old upside-down plastic crate; Miguel's back as he stood in front of the toilet, not bothering to shut the door behind him when he had to go. The air was stale, the decor empty. There was hardly any furniture. I remember how, in the mornings, Yvette was allowed to leave the bedroom, to sit on the floor of the living room with Apple Jacks and cartoons. I, on the other hand, wasn't allowed to go out and be with my sister. I wanted to, but Jose Sr. wouldn't let me out of the bedroom. I hated being alone with him. I didn't know if I had done something wrong, or if I was being punished, or why. And I didn't understand why Ruth just left us with him. I don't remember one happy moment there at all.

Thankfully, it didn't last long. One day, I heard an argument between Ruth and Jose Sr. I didn't see her, but I could hear her voice mix with his as the two of them screamed at one another. And then the door slammed shut, and then I was told that someone was going to pick me up and take me back to my parents' house. *Finally,* I thought, *I'm getting out of here!*

IT WAS in first grade when things started to change. I was a little bit older than the other kids, that was true—but there was something more. I noticed that my classmates saw me as different. And I saw myself as different, too.

It wasn't like that in my prekindergarten class. In the mornings, when Mami helped me get ready, I'd eat breakfast, brush my teeth, and put on my uniform of dark blue pants, white shirt, and black tie. I never once dreaded taking the yellow bus to my special school in Washington Heights. I liked the other kids. We colored and played, and I didn't even mind nap time.

But by the time I was in first grade at PS 56, I was more self-conscious, more aware that I was not like the other kids in my class. During recess, the other kids teased me.

"Why do you walk like that?"

"Why do you talk like that?"

"Why are you always with the girls?"

"Josephina!"

It got worse as I got older. After school, I took the shortcut through Oval Park. But these older boys who lived in the brick house on the corner sat on their porch and called me names as I walked by.

"Faggot!"

"What's wrong with you?"

I didn't really understand what they were asking. I tried to ignore these kinds of questions. I tried not to let these words get to me. I walked quickly through the park, past other kids climbing up the playscapes and my brothers on the basketball court. I liked it there, and though I wanted to play with the others, I didn't want them to start making fun of me, too. I didn't want the park to be a place where I'd be bullied or made to feel unsafe. I didn't want to stop going there because I was afraid of what kids would say to me. And so I kept to myself. I tried to think about all that had happened at school, to get it all out before I got home. When I made it to the tunnel at the far end of the park, I raised my face and let out a long "haaa-oooohh!" I loved hearing my voice crisp and clear, echoing. I turned the corner and saw the old farmhouse museum and was filled with a sense of relief: I was almost home.

SOMETIMES, I did wonder: *Is there something wrong with me?* I just wanted to be one of the girls, like Seli, or Isa, or Elsa—the pretty Mexican girl in my class with the long straight black hair. But slowly, I realized that this was impossible. That I was only dreaming. At home, in my room, it was a relief to be alone. To be able to wear Seli's clothes. To play with one of Isa's forgotten Barbies. To not have anyone question me. I looked out my window onto the park and tried to imagine what it would be like if I had just been born a girl. This was my little escape. The place where I could be myself, experiment with makeup and clothes and listen to music loud. I was infatuated with Shakira then, and I'd belly dance in front of the mirror, my hair wrapped. But even then, behind my locked door, I was nervous that someone would come in. All you needed was a bobby pin to pop the lock from the outside, and sometimes Isa would bust in, without as little as a knock. I'd try to cover myself up, to tell her to get out, that I was changing and needed privacy! But I knew that, eventually, I'd have to come back to my reality: that because of the body I'd been born into, these things must be kept secret from everyone else.

Isa got to do all the things I wanted to do. She played with Barbies. She could wear dresses and skirts and grow her hair long. When we played house, she insisted that I be the daddy.

"Can't I be the mommy or the sister?" I asked.

"No, you're a boy!"

"Fine." But in my mind, I was the mommy. I slipped on Seli's pink fuzzy slippers and carried baby dolls in my arms, feeding them, burping them.

"No, you're doing it wrong! That's not how the daddy does it!"

Why couldn't Isa just let me be? I wished that she was more like Seli, that she would just let me have fun. Isa never wanted to play with her girly toys—it was only when I wanted to play with them that she'd get possessive. In her room, she had a big blue-and-white-striped laundry bag full of Barbies and their accessories that she hardly touched. I'd go in and open the bag to take Barbies out to play. When she saw me playing with her things, she'd throw a fit. "Noooooooo, that's mine! Mami!"

Oh no, I'd think. *Here we go.*

Mami would come and see what I was doing, and sigh. "Well, they are Isa's things. And if she doesn't want you playing with it, then you can't."

Sometimes, Isa would want me to play Barbies with her, and I'd get so excited. *Yes, finally!* I'd always go all-in, picking out the cutest clothes and accessories. Things would be okay for a minute, until Isa saw how cute my Barbie looked. Then, she'd snatch it out of my hands. "You're not supposed to be playing with it anyways," she'd say. "This one is my Barbie." So I'd pick up another and make her outfit even cuter. And Isa'd notice and snatch that one away too.

I couldn't wait for Seli to get home. But when she was home, she needed to practice her lines. I begged her to let me be in her room with her.

"No! I need some time alone."

"Please?" I asked. "Can't I just watch?!"

"You can't be here right now," she said, locking me out.

I waited out in the hallway for her to let me in. I tried to be very patient. But every few minutes I'd give a little knock, just to remind her that I was still there. Eventually, in my frustration, I went back to my room. I found one of Isa's old Barbies that I hid under my bed, and I used scissors to cut off all of her long, straight yellow hair.

MY BROTHERS—THEY tried to toughen me up. They'd dress me up in football gear and take me to the park, where they tried to show me what it was like to be a boy. It always felt wrong to me, what they were doing, and now I know that it is impossible to change one's natural tendencies or gender identity through violence and intimidation. But at the time, they thought that this was the way to make me stronger, to man me up. One day, my brothers and their friend Ricky decided to stage a fight between me and Ricky's little brother, who was my age but bigger and tougher. They stood us in front of one another at the bottom of the slope we'd sled down in winter and formed a circle around us. And then, the taunts began.

"Jose, you better fuck him up!"

"Hit him, Jose!"

"Punch his lights out!"

But I couldn't hit anyone. I was fragile. I was terrified to fight. I didn't want to raise a punch. And I couldn't understand why my brothers were putting me, who always acted and felt like a little girl, up against a boy. It didn't seem fair. And so I just stood there, frozen, scared for my life.

Please, can't I just go home and be with Seli? I wanted to ask.

And then I felt it: a fist against my face. And another. And another. I was bleeding and could already feel where my lip and eyebrow would bruise and swell.

I didn't really talk about what happened that day. I remember, when I got home, Mami asking me what had happened. I shrugged and told her that I was just at the park with Tony and Tito and their friends. My brothers had broken us apart before too long, before I was hurt real bad, but the damage was already done.

When I was around ten, Mami told me that I needed to get a passport.

"*Vamos a visitar a tu papa Jose en Santo Domingo.*"

"NO!" I responded. "Mami, *no quiero ir.*"

"Jose," she explained. "*Tenemos que ir, el te quiere ver.*"

I didn't understand why my biological father wanted to see me. I never wanted to talk to Jose Sr., and sometimes, when he'd call, Mami and Papi told him I wasn't there. Other times, they'd make me talk to him, just to say hello. But now, in retrospect, I think that my parents felt like they needed to keep Ruth and Jose Sr. happy. I think Mami and Papi were afraid that if they didn't, I would be taken away from them again. The moment Mami told me about the trip, however, my anxiety grew.

DR was like nothing I'd ever seen before. In my memory, the floors and roads were all made of dirt. Mami and I arrived at the prison, which was ugly and dark, and the guards checked us in. I didn't want anything to do with Jose Sr., so I tried not to pay too much attention, but I remember noticing the metal bars.

And then I heard him: "*Bendicion,* Papi."

His voice made me cringe. I became angry and started to shut down and go numb. I stood there straight-faced, not saying anything. Mami spoke to me softly, telling me to say hi, to be nice. I greeted him, but after that I didn't say anything more. I thought, *I'm gonna be cold.* Mami didn't seem to notice or care, and thankfully, the visit was short. Afterward, we went to visit my biological grandmother. She lived on farmland, in the campo, and I kept my distance from her, too. Mami talked to her, but I didn't know what they were saying.

I asked to use the bathroom, and my grandmother pointed down the hall. When I closed the door, I saw that the toilet was nothing like I was used to. Instead, it was a metal tube that reminded me of a coffee canister, set into a hole in the ground.

TOWARD THE end of the year, when I was in third grade, my teacher Miss Lopez had us do a math project with colored paper and scissors. I finished my assignment early, and so I sat there quietly sorting and tidying and making patterns with the colorful scraps. I took one, a long strip, and twisted it around my finger. I taped the coil onto my head and let it hang like a curl. The kids around me all started laughing. "Oh my God—what are you doing?" They shouted, "You're not a girl!" Their voices steadily grew louder and louder, until Miss Lopez snapped.

She pulled me out into the hallway. "You cannot do that," she said. "You're distracting the other kids from learning."

I wasn't sure what she meant. I wasn't trying to distract anyone—I was just playing with my hair! But I never did anything like this again, and teasing voices and whispers started following me in the hallways. *Faggot!* They'd say. *Is that a girl?*

When school started the next year, and I was in the fourth grade, I realized that Miss Lopez made a request to have me placed in the special education class. Maybe part of her thought that I needed this, that it would be a better environment for me to learn in; but I can't help but feel that part of her simply didn't want that kind of energy— my energy—in the general education classes. At the time, I thought that maybe this smaller class would be better, that maybe these kids wouldn't be as hurtful or mean. But very quickly I found that it was all the same. I wondered if I'd ever feel comfortable to be myself in front of others.

Chapter 4

SELENIS & MARIZOL

. . . .

I wish I could draw the scene: Christmas morning. The tree decorated and lit, the living room filled with wrapping paper. We've all had breakfast, and everyone's excited and loud and opening presents. And here's Jose, three years old, in his red one-piece pajamas, sitting in the middle of it all. He's opened a gift, maybe two, but the rest sit untouched.

You know how kids are. Ripping through the wrapping and the ribbons with excitement. Delighted by one gift and then on to the next.

"Yay! It's Christmas!"

But not Jose. He's straining to see what I'm opening, what Isa is opening. I think that every year he had hope. But every year, it was always the same: after he opened those first gifts, his eyes seemed to say, "Yep, all the same bullshit. I don't want any of this." The look of excitement he had earlier that morning quickly left his face. And it was replaced by a look I've come to know all too well over the years: a look of longing.

. . . .

A BARBIE with long hair—that's what I wanted. Or a baby doll I could hold like Isa held hers. Maybe pink fluffy slippers like Seli had, like the ones I liked to wear when no one else was around. I loved the way they felt on my feet. With my wrapped gifts laid out in front of me, I closed my eyes and imagined all of my secret dreams coming true.

I opened the first present: a truck. The next: a football. I shoved the boxes aside and waited for Isa to open hers. A Barbie. A stuffed white dog with a cute bow. A baby doll. I didn't want everyone to know how excited I was about her gifts, so I tried to control myself. But I really wanted to grab them! Everything was pink, pretty—and not mine. I held one of her dolls, running my fingers through her hair. I imagined how I would change her clothes, and I reached for her little brush.

"Leave her alone!" Isa screamed. "It's mine! You have your own presents!"

I just wanted to see what she got! I just wanted to play with them for a minute! But she didn't want to share.

. . . .

I COULD SEE that Jose was embarrassed. He pretended to enjoy his own toys, but I saw the disappointment in his eyes—and I wished I could have done something to make him happy. Even now, I wish that, just once, I'd gotten him a Barbie.

. . . .

I WAS excited when I opened the Game Boy. *Okay, this is something I like!* It was blue and smooth in my hands. I told Mami and Papi, "Thank you." I looked over at Isa, wanting to show her my cool new toy. But I saw that she got a Game Boy, too, and right away I wanted to trade. I could take hers, and she could take mine.

Why not? Why couldn't mine be pink?

Chapter 5

MARIZOL

. . . .

Seli always had the prettiest shoes. And so many of them. I remember her coming home from a long day of shoe shopping, walking around the house to flaunt her new heels. I loved the sound they made, that assertive little *click* against the hardwood floor. I was infatuated with Seli—her presence, her style, her femininity. And I wanted to do it, too: to be all fancy, to have my feet delicately arched in the air.

The nicest shoes she kept in pairs, neatly arranged in a shoe rack on the inside of her closet door. Others were thrown in the back of the closet, one shoe's match sometimes hard to find. I knew that I shouldn't touch the ones on the rack, but the ones in the back felt like safer bets. They weren't organized, and so she'd never know if they weren't back in the exact right place. Or, at least, that's what I hoped. But sometimes, I wondered if she knew how I'd sneak into her room while she wasn't home, trying on her heels, her sandals, her flats. I worried she'd figure out that something was different and know right away that it was me. I wasn't the only one who did this, though— often, Isa would try on Seli's shoes with me.

We always noticed the new pairs right away. One time: leather platform heels that were black and strappy, maybe six inches high. We each put one shoe on and stood, our bare feet hovering off the floor as we tried to balance.

Another time, we were going through the closet not in her bedroom but along the porch, where Mami and Papi kept the out-of-season coats and fancier clothes. Though the closet is large, Isa and I didn't have the space to walk around like we did in Seli's room—and if we walked out onto the porch, we risked getting caught. For Isa, she would have been caught doing something she shouldn't be doing: trying on Seli's clothes without her permission. For me, it was the same but also something much worse. For me, there was an embarrassment, a kind of shame. So we shut the door and turned on the light. Mami and Seli had a wedding to go to the next day and everything had been set out and ironed. And that was when we saw them: Seli's shoes for the wedding. They were beige and strappy and had a tall, skinny heel. I put one on, and Isa the other, and we hobbled around the narrow space, amazed at how the shoes looked on our feet.

And then I heard a crack. I felt something go sideways and break. I stumbled and saw that the heel of the shoe had completely broken off.

"Oh my God!" I said. "What are we gonna do? Seli's gonna kill us."

"Not me," Isa said. "You're the one who broke it."

"Promise me you won't say it was me. Isa, please? Promise?"

She looked at the shoe, and then at me, and sighed. "Fine. But put it back—let's get out of here."

We left the closet and everything in it as we found it—except for that one broken shoe. I knew that Seli was going to be home soon, and so I went to my room to try to calm myself. *Maybe, I should just pretend to be sleeping,* I thought. *That way, when she comes home and finds it, I'll have an excuse.*

Just a few minutes later, it seemed, my sister came storming into my room. My bed was lofted and next to the door, so when she pushed the door open her face was right next to mine. I tried to steady my breathing, to look like I was sleeping.

"I know you're awake," she said.

She doesn't know, I thought. *I could be asleep.*

"Jose," she said, shaking me. "Jose."

Keep calm. Try not to smile.

"Isa told me everything!"

And that's when I couldn't hold it in any longer. My eyes darted open.

Seli went on: "I can't believe you broke my shoe!"

"It wasn't me!" I said. "I swear it wasn't me!"

"It was you," she said. "I know it was you. What am I supposed to do for this wedding tomorrow?"

She turned and left, slamming the door behind her, leaving me on my bed.

Oh my God, I thought. Of course I didn't mean to break it! I was just doing something I knew would feed my soul, something that would make me feel good. I wasn't a little kid anymore—it had been a long time since I'd done Seli's hair when she came home from school—and I was exploring more and more things that could make me feel whole. But I felt like I couldn't be open about those things, not even with Seli. And so even though I felt bad about making Seli mad, I couldn't help but worry about the bigger problem now that my secret of trying on her shoes was out: *Is Seli gonna think different about me now?* I was scared as hell.

I **NEVER** told anyone at home about what the other kids at school said to me or how I was teased. Not Mami, not Papi, not even Seli. At the time, I didn't really know why I didn't say anything. Now, I think that part of me was afraid that if they heard those things, they would start to think that way about me, too.

But of course they could sense that something was wrong. Isa went to the same school as me, so she knew. She knew, but we never talked about what it was like to be bullied all the time or how it made me feel. Sometimes, though, she'd tell me how the kids in her class would come up to her and ask her questions about me: "Why is your brother gay?" or "Why is he always hanging around the girls?" I know that she hated this, that it frustrated her to make excuses for me. But Isa was tough, and fiercely loyal. Family has always been big for her, and if anyone said anything about me or someone else in our family, she wasn't afraid to shove them, to put them in their place. And this—despite all of the fighting we'd do at home and all of the competition that existed between us—was comforting.

After I graduated from the fifth grade, Mami asked me if I wanted to go to St. Brendan's, a private school connected to our church. It was across the street from my elementary school, so I passed by it every day. I remember thinking that the kids who went there didn't have backpacks—they had luggage. Rolling bags that were overstuffed with books. Probably more books for one semester than I would've used for all three years at Middle School 80.

"What do you think?" she asked.

But more than the hours of homework I imagined the students had each night, what stuck out to me was that it was a religious school. One that was very strict. One that probably wouldn't approve of someone like me.

"Nah, I don't wanna go to that school," I said.

She shrugged, and after a short summer, I began sixth grade at Middle School 80. And there, I tried even harder to blend in, to not be noticed.

MS 80 was just a few blocks from my house, and every morning the kids lined up outside, on the basketball courts, waiting for the bell to ring and the doors to open. At first, I got to school early. But I didn't like being part of a crowd. I didn't want to be around so many people. I didn't want to give anyone the chance of calling me out. And so I started showing up later and later, after everyone else was already inside. After school, it was the same story. I took the back way home, walking alone down the quiet streets so that nobody could say anything to me. I stayed as far away as I could from those fuckers, but I couldn't always avoid them.

There was this one kid, Shaun, who always called me names. I tried to make myself small, to blend in, but when he'd pass me in the hallways, he gave me shit.

"You better get out of my way, faggot," he said. "Or I'll fuck you up."

"What the fuck you talking about?" I said. "I'm not gay."

"Oh you wanna go?" he said, raising his arms and puffing up his chest.

Luckily, the bell rang, and I rushed into my classroom before things got worse.

But even in class, he was ready to pick on me. I always felt uneasy around him, worried about what he'd say or do. And it started to impact my learning. If I raised my hand to answer a question or to speak up in class, he'd repeat what I'd say in a high-pitched, feminine voice. It was the simplest form of teasing, but it was constant, and it hit me right where I was the most vulnerable. I became silent more and more in class.

I wasn't the only one who got bullied at school. My friend Justin got bullied, too.

"Fag!"

"Are you gay?"

"Are you a boy or a girl?"

But Justin was much more comfortable, much more out there than I was. He wore tight clothes. He walked confidently down the hallway like a girl who knew she was fine.

I could never act like that, I thought, in awe of his confidence. Instead, I was just backing away, tryna cover myself up. Tryn' not to be bullied as much. I kept my distance from Justin at school so that nobody would question why I was hanging out with someone so flamboyant. For the yearly talent show, he performed "Toxic" by Britney Spears full out. He crawled on the ground all sexy-like, flashed his hands around his face like she does in the music video. Some kids laughed, but most of them cheered him on. Everyone was expecting something like this from him, but I'd never imagined someone could be so open, so free.

ANOTHER BIRTHDAY was coming, and it was a big one: my sixteenth.

After school, I used to watch the MTV show *My Super Sweet Sixteen;* by the time I was in the eighth grade, it was one of my favorites, one of the few things that helped me forget how awkward and out of place I felt. When it was on, I could enter a kind of fantasy world, one with princess gowns and tiaras and rhinestone-studded shoes.

So when Mami asked me what I wanted for my sixteenth birthday, I told her: a party. In a big venue, disco ball boomin', the dance floor packed with kids from my school having the time of their lives—the whole nine.

I knew I couldn't dress like the girls from the show at my own party. I knew I couldn't get my makeup or nails done. It was weird enough for a guy in my neighborhood to have a birthday party at all. But I needed this party. This party was gonna make me feel good. I didn't tell anyone, but the truth was: this party was going to make me feel like *me*.

"Let me talk to Papi," Mami said.

El Coral was a restaurant just two short blocks from our house, next to Mami's nail salon and the bodega. It wasn't a place any of us really knew about or went to, but at the time it was one of the only Latin bars around. (All of the other bars, farther down the avenue, were Irish pubs.) I'd heard that there was a private event space upstairs, and after finding out what it would cost to have the party there, Papi agreed.

"Oh my God!" I said to them. "I have the best parents ever!"

I thought, *This is gonna be the shit!*

I didn't call it a Sweet Sixteen because I knew that was going to be too obvious, so I called it a Sixteen Bash. I had so much fun with the whole process: the planning, passing out the invites at school. Because I was a few years older than most of my classmates, I was excited that I was going to be the first to have a party like this. I remember sitting with Seli on the couch, flipping through a catalog she had that sold party supplies and decorations. At first I wanted something Hollywood-themed, like a Red Carpet Affair. I'd bought these cute black-tie invitations at the ninety-nine cents store, and I used those to invite around fifty people. But then in the catalog I saw this package for a Mardi Gras party, with masks and beads and glittery streamers, and I was sold. We ordered a cake—half guava, half custard—from our family's spot, the legendary bakery Resposteria Nitin. Everything was purple, green, gold.

At school, I was keeping things low-key so that no one would suspect anything of me. I did things I thought a regular guy would do. I wore loose-fitting pants and kept my hair short. I even had a girlfriend. A student at St. Brendan's, she was pretty and shy, with long, curly hair. But it was like wearing an outfit that doesn't fit. I always felt uncomfortable in my clothes, awkward with her. But this party was an excuse to let things go a little. To be flashy. To celebrate me. I talked the party up! And the kids at school all seemed excited, saying that they'd be there. Still, part of me knew I couldn't be too out there. I couldn't risk being found out. And so I didn't invite Justin. Because what would the other kids suspect about me if I invited someone as out there as he was?

The day of the party, I played the diva. Tony took me to get a haircut and hooked me up with a white Lacoste shirt. I didn't get my nails or makeup done like I wanted to, but I went to Nancy, Mami's nail lady, and she waxed my eyebrows for the first time.

Seli and Gina, one of my cousins, hooked the party hall up with decorations. Colored lights were flashin'. Trays and trays of food—rice and pepper steak, lasagna, salad—were set up banquet style in the front of the room, and tables and chairs circled the dance floor. The cake was in the back, beside the DJ, in front of shiny, metallic curtains that hung from the ceiling. With the music playing and the lights going, it was like my own private club.

At first, it was just my family there. Mami and Papi, my siblings, a few cousins. Kimberly, the girl who lived below us, came with her brother and cousins. We were all dancing, having a good time, but I was distracted. I was wondering when everyone else was gonna show. My girlfriend came, but not for long. She was dressed up, looking all grown in her mom's high-heeled boots, some tight pants, and an open-back top. She hadn't told her parents about the party, or about me, and just a few minutes after she showed, her mom stormed up the stairs. She talked to Mami in quick Spanish, and then dragged her daughter home. I'm sure she got into some real trouble that night, but to be honest, I was kind of relieved when she left; I was afraid that my family was gonna be watching us together, that I was gonna have to put on a show.

I started texting my friends from school on my Sidekick.

Yo, you coming to my party?
Yeah, we'll be there!

But the minutes just ticked on by. *Why did hardly anyone show?* I wondered. *Is it because they can tell what I really am?* I tried not to look sad, but I felt so bad for Mami and Papi. They put so much money and effort into making this party just how I wanted. And it was—but without the huge crowd, without dozens of kids from my school trying to get close to me on the dance floor.

I started to feel really low. *Damn,* I thought. But when I looked around at those who were there, a feeling of happiness washed over me. My sisters and cousins and neighbors were dressed up and dancing. Mami and Papi had thrown me a party. My immediate people, the ones who really loved me, were there. I got my party, and I was grateful for that. I joined my family on the dance floor and thought to all who didn't come, *Y'all are the ones who lost.*

"**YOU BETTER** watch yourself, faggot!"

The bell had rung, and the hallway was nearly empty. I turned around and saw Shaun standing in front of a row of lockers.

"Shut the fuck up," I said.

"What did you say to me, homo?"

"I'm not gay. And you fucking heard me."

On most days, I'd have been walking away by this point. I'd have been afraid of getting in a fight, of having my ass kicked. But something that day told me to hold my ground.

When I went to school the day after my party, I asked my so-called friends why they never showed. "My grandmother was sick." Or, "My mom wouldn't let me." I didn't question them, but deep inside I was asking: *Come on, really?* I tried to push it to the back of my mind. I even lied about how poppin' it was. "Mad people came," I said. "It was so much fun! Y'all missed out!"

I think the experience of being let down at my party and of all of the frustrations that had been building up over the years from constantly being bullied finally caused me to reach a breaking point. That day in the hallway, I decided that I'd just had enough. I was gonna defend myself.

Shaun walked up to me slowly. Then he grabbed my shoulders and head and put me into a headlock. Somehow, I got out of it, and I saw an anger swell inside of him that I'd never seen before. He lunged toward me again, headbutting his forehead against mine. *He's really trying to hurt me,* I thought. *He's going to fuck me up.*

Instead of being scared, this realization gave me fuel, and I was furious in a way I can never remember being before. Something inside me snapped. The next thing I knew I had his shoulders between my hands. I pushed him up against the gray-blue lockers, and I started banging his head against their small metal doors. And I didn't stop. I just kept slamming the back of his head, over and over and over, into the lockers. I wasn't just hitting Shaun, who made my life at MS 80 a living hell, but I was hitting everyone who'd made fun of me over the years. Everyone who'd called me names. Everyone who'd lied to me about coming to my party. It wasn't long before I blacked out, letting my anger and frustration and rage take me over entirely.

Eventually, teachers and other students came out into the hallway to see what all the commotion was. My teacher, the teacher next door, my counselor, someone from the dean's office—they all came rushing toward us and pulled me off of him. When I came to my senses, I was shaking. I looked up at him and saw the shock on his face. He didn't know I was capable of reacting that way—and neither did I.

This isn't me, I thought. I was afraid of what I'd done, of what I realized I was capable of.

My brother Tony came to pick me up early from school that day. I was afraid of what was gonna happen next, that I was gonna be in trouble for fighting, for getting sent home. But as we were walking, he asked me about what happened and I told him. We stopped in the middle of the sidewalk, and he looked at me and grabbed my shoulder. "Good," he said. "You handled it good."

Chapter 6

SELENIS

. . . .

Around the time Jose was in middle school, we received news that Ruth had passed. My mother didn't know how to address the news or how to tell Jose. I told her that I would handle it. I wonder now why I offered. I think I wanted to protect my mother from discomfort and sadness. I also believed that I could deliver the news in a way that would allow Jose to open up to me.

As to the specifics of where we were, my memory fails me. All I can remember is a stillness that engulfed the two of us in that moment.

"I'm really sorry to have to tell you this," I said softly. "We heard today that Ruth died."

Silence.

"It's okay to be sad," I said.

Again: silence.

"Do you want to talk about it?"

He didn't speak but instead said no with a small shake of his head. I could see water pool in his eyes and a look of confusion take over his face. Now, I know that this is the look of a child in the midst of processing terrible news. A look of sadness and confusion and disbelief.

The next day, I tried to get him to open up again.

"How are you feeling? Are you sad?"

This time, he spoke. But it was nothing more than a quick "no" before changing the subject. I suspected that there was a lot more behind that single word, but I didn't push it. I will admit, though I am ashamed to do so, that in that moment I felt relief. Ruth was gone, as was the threat of her taking him away from us.

DURING THOSE YEARS, I belonged to a comedy troupe called Nuyorican Rule. We performed once a month at the Nuyorican Poets Cafe in the Lower East Side. I wasn't earning financially, but I was earning in experience. It was a time of tremendous growth for me as an artist. Comedy is not easy! You have to be quick and ready, and I loved it. We wrote our own material, and we were responsible for our own costumes and props. So it was normal to walk into my room then and see a collection of wigs, everything from straight blond to full afro. I kept a wicker trunk filled with my comedy collection. And every so often, things would just go missing. If I couldn't find a blouse, or a necklace, or a costume for a performance, I knew where it was. I knew who had it. And I didn't make a big deal out of it.

Let Jose do what he needs to do, I thought.

Sometimes, when getting ready for an audition or a night out, I wouldn't be able to find a specific top or pair of shoes. I'd roll my eyes and sigh. "Come *on*! Why does it have to be *that* shirt?!" But I never asked, I just let it be. The only time I ever confronted Jose was the night before the wedding, when he broke my shoe. All this time, through all of the missing clothes and accessories, I felt like I was supporting Jose in my own little way. I was turning the other cheek. Pretending like nothing was happening. And there he went, breaking my shoe. Over time, I learned to hide the things I really loved.

Nothing he took was lost forever; eventually, things resurfaced. Sometimes, if I was desperate, I'd go into his room and search way in the back of his closet or under his bed—and there it would be. It didn't take long for me to become familiar with all the hiding places. Other times, my mother would find things I'd been looking for—stockings, a dress, a gaudy jeweled necklace. She would come running out of the room and say to me, "*¿Mira, tu no estaba buscando esto?*"

She and I had an understanding: We wouldn't make a big deal about it to others. We didn't outright speak about it, just as we never spoke about how we interpreted Jose's femininity as being gay, but it was something that was clear between the two of us.

But what I didn't know: Was dressing up in women's clothes a normal thing for a gay man to do? I wasn't sure, and so I talked about Jose and his habits with a close friend of mine from the theater. He laughed.

"Oh, hunnie," he said. "You know, I used to put my mother's rollers or pins in my hair—that's just what we do!"

I accepted this and believed it to be true—but I also knew that there was something more. That there was something about Jose's essence that was more than being gay.

ONE DAY, WHEN Jose was in the eighth grade, he introduced me to his girlfriend.

Your *what?!* I wanted to ask. Instead, I was polite and smiled as I reached to shake her hand.

"Oh, hi! It's good to meet you," I said.

Jose was giggling, trying to hide his face. "Oh my God, what?! Seli!" He looked like the cat who just ate the canary.

He and I both knew this was not real. And I'm pretty sure that the girl, deep down, knew as well. She was pretty, short and cute with long reddish hair and a shy expression on her face. *Oh, girl,* I thought to myself, *please don't fall for him.*

But the way they hung around each other—it was clear they weren't boyfriend-and-girlfriend. They were just friends, and Jose wouldn't look at me without grinning or laughing.

Well, this is cute, I thought.

WHEN JOSE ANNOUNCED that he wanted a birthday party, I knew what he had in mind: a Sweet Sixteen and all that comes with it. But in our small, close-knit neighborhood in the Bronx, boys didn't have Sweet Sixteens. They rarely had birthday parties. I remember my brothers hearing the news and asking, "He wants *what?*"

My own sixteenth birthday party was a production, one that took an entire year to plan. I organized rehearsals with my friends and cousins—sixteen couples in total. They came to my house for months before the event to practice the dance routines I'd planned for the big day. The waltz, the Hustle, a dance with my boyfriend, the father-daughter dance. My dress was literally a wedding dress. When I first tried it on, I fell in love—it was massive, with lots of lace and plenty of tulle for pouf. I paired it with white gloves and a tiara Mami and I purchased at a bridal store in downtown Manhattan, and I wore ballerina slippers.

Before the party, there was church ceremony for the blessing, a professional photographer, limos. We had over two hundred guests. Then there were speeches, tears, a DJ, and hours and hours of dancing. To symbolize my entering into womanhood, my father removed my ballerina slippers and replaced them with white heels. We then danced our father-daughter dance together. I remember feeling so happy. So special. I was growing up, becoming the woman I'd always wanted to be.

Jose's party wasn't that. Jose's party was lacking. Jose's party was sad.

My cousin and I decorated the hall while Jose got himself ready. We hung streamers and scattered Mardi Gras beads on the tables. When we finished, we were proud of our work. We were happy to make something special for Jose, my baby brother.

I'll never forget how cute Jose looked in his baggy pants and white collared shirt, his hair freshly cut and in a fade. He got his eyebrows done that day, too—yet another thing boys in our neighborhood did not regularly do. They were still thick, but angled and defined. Looking back, I see how restrained Jose was in this moment. Here he was, at this party that he'd wanted, but still unable to fully *be*. It was Mardi Gras after all! And this was supposed to be a Sweet Sixteen! I know that he had envisioned something else.

Of course we all had a good time, the whole family together, dressed up and dancing. But here we were, with a DJ and a buffet, in a huge room with hardly anyone to fill it. We had prepared a party for a big crowd of teenagers, and in my head I had hoped that it would be packed, filled with people celebrating him. Our family was there, and our neighbors in the unit below. Jose's "girlfriend" was there for a short time, too, before her mother came and dragged her home. But that was it. No one from Jose's school. I looked over at Jose, the Mardi Gras beads around his neck glistening against his white shirt, and watched as he glanced toward the entrance. I saw his smile vanish, just for a second, as he realized that no one else would be coming through that door. I remember, hours into the party, looking around the room and it suddenly seeming bigger. The decorations were up and the lights were going, but the majority of tables remained untouched. Jose didn't have a lot of friends, and I knew that, but seeing him there, surrounded not by people but by empty space—that broke my heart. And though I couldn't quite put my finger on it at the time, I could tell that my baby brother was not happy.

The party reminded me of all of those other moments I'd noticed throughout the years—moments that should have been filled with excitement and joy: every Christmas morning, every birthday, every celebration, every day that he was forced to feign being happy and content. *Here we go again*, I thought. I wished that things could have been different for him. I wished that I could have done something. *If I had a magic wand, I would stop everything for Jose to have that moment for him to just fully be free. To have a room filled with friends, all accepting of him. To finally be who he longs to be.*

Of course, I didn't have a magic wand. And neither did anyone else in the family. I think that everyone in that room noticed

Jose's disappointment, but none of us said anything about it. None of us wanted to make a big deal about how uncomfortable it must have been for him. And so we danced. We ate the food. We made the best of the situation in the only way we knew how.

I'm grateful that we banded together to celebrate this human being whom we loved so much. It was by no means perfect. We all recognized that Jose was going through identity issues; this was an unspoken truth in our family. And though I wonder now what things might have been like if we had been able to speak more openly about it, I also know that we all used our individual knowledge and tools to show him love and support. So many trans youth lack support from their families. And for trans youth of color, the feeling of isolation, of rejection, can be much worse.

As a mother, I've learned how hard it can be to bring up uncomfortable issues with our children. But we need to face our own fears and be there for them when they need us. We need to be there for our children, no matter how they identify. We need to be there for them even if we don't quite know how. We need them to know that, no matter who they are, they are important to our community. We need them to know that their lives matter and should be celebrated.

Being there for our children also means that we have a responsibility to teach them acceptance, self-love, and respect for others—regardless of whether we share the same worldviews or not. One of the most shocking things I've seen is how many parents fail to see how their own behavior and actions affect their children. Acts of hate and discrimination are not innate to our existence as human beings; these are learned behaviors. I have watched bullies get complete support from their parents, who ignore their child's actions, make excuses, or even blame the victim! We, as parents, need to recognize this fact, become accountable for the actions of our children. We need to teach them how profound an impact their words and behaviors can have on the life of another.

Chapter 7

MARIZOL

· · · · · · · · · ·

You know that feeling a lot of people have when they are little, that feeling of being excited to grow up, to move on to the next thing? In preschool, you're excited for elementary. In elementary, you're excited for middle school. In middle school, you can't wait to get to high school.

It wasn't like that for me.

For so much of my life, I knew I was different. I knew what it felt like—I knew what it *looked* like—to be different. Before I started high school, I worried that I wouldn't make friends. I was scared that I'd be bullied, that I'd be singled out again. I wanted to do good in school, to graduate, to have the kinds of opportunities that only a high school diploma could bring. And I knew that I was on my way to accomplishing something important. But instead of enjoying the process of moving on to something new, the back of my head was always clouded with anxieties, with what-if's.

I decided not to go to the neighborhood high school, the big school where my brothers went. They straight up told me not to. This was for a lot of reasons: the school was big, the teachers weren't good, so on and so on. But I couldn't help but wonder: *Do they know how much of an outcast I am? That, there, I'll just be a target?*

I ended up going to a smaller school called Wings Academy, which was a few miles away. Every day, I took the bus to Gun Hill Road, where I got on the 2 or 4 train to East 180th Street. I hoped that someone from my middle school would go there, but it was just me. In some ways, I knew that I should make a fresh start, take this as an opportunity to start showing people the real me. But I always worried—what if they didn't like the real me?—and so I kept to myself. I tried to do all I could to blend in, to just be a regular teenager. I tried to hide who I was, and I was so uncomfortable. Looking back on it now, I realize that so much of my time was spent trying to ignore my discomfort or avoid situations that made me uneasy. I hoped that I could just make it through the day without an incident.

The bathroom was always a huge source of anxiety for me. I hated using the boys' bathroom. I knew that guys would play around, bust in on one another in the stalls, and I didn't want to be caught up in that. At first, I tried to avoid using the bathroom at all costs, but that just wasn't realistic. Then, I tried to avoid going during times I knew it'd be busy, like passing time or lunch. But still, even when I went during class, I always feared that another guy would be in there, waiting to say something to me, or burst in on me while I was in the stall, or worse.

Giving transgender folk access to the public restrooms that match their gender identity has become a huge concern for many Americans and lawmakers. But when it comes down to it, I want people to understand that we, transgender individuals, are just like everyone else. We want to be able to use the bathroom in peace, to feel safe and secure as we go about our business. We are not trying to harm others or entering bathrooms with dangerous intentions. Unfortunately, many believe the opposite about transgender individuals, and this is a direct result of how we have been stigmatized and portrayed negatively in the media.

Even to this day, I worry about what is going to happen for me in a public restroom. I worry that someone is going to spook me or make a scene. But in high school, before I transitioned, my fears were much worse. Eventually, if I really had to go, I learned that I could use the single-stall bathroom upstairs, the one specifically meant for staff. All I had to do was ask the front-office secretary for the key. She never questioned me or told me that it wasn't allowed; instead, she was kind and compassionate. I think that she could sense that I was different and saw me for me. During lunchtime, she helped monitor the cafeteria, keeping order and excusing tables once the period had ended. I'm sure she saw how I was teased. How I always felt alone.

Bathrooms weren't my only source of stress at school. I had similar anxieties about gym and changing in the locker room. Every year, we got to choose between dance and physical education. I really wanted to take dance, but it was mostly all girls—there may have been a couple of guys, but I was scared what other people would say about me. If they'd make fun of how I danced. If they'd call me names for doing an activity that was mainly for girls.

In middle school, Seli had put me in classes at Alvin Ailey. I liked it at first. I was starting to accept the fact that it wasn't sustainable for me to always try to hide who I was. Dancing was a way for me to let go, and I was quick to pick up the moves. One of my instructors, though, was especially tough on me. Maybe she knew I had potential and wanted to push me to the next level. But instead of motivating me to try harder, this kind of attention just made me feel self-conscious. I felt like all eyes were on me, and it reminded me of the constant stares I got at school or walking down the street. And more than feeling self-conscious, I remember feeling envious of the other kids who were comfortable in their own skin and could just let it all go. I started to worry about what these confident, talented kids would think about someone like me, so I stopped going. And in high school, it was the same shit: me not doing what I really wanted because I was scared of how others would see me.

So, instead of choosing dance, I chose gym. I had the option of doing weight lifting, but it was all the masculine-type guys. Too much testosterone. I knew I wouldn't fit in there, either, so I stuck with the normal gym class, where I could blend in better.

At first, it was okay. Our school was small, without a regulation-sized track, and the principal was hesitant about letting us run around outside. Instead, my gym teacher had us walk or jog in the hallway that circled the gymnasium. During these activities, nobody said nothing to me. But when we started playing basketball or volleyball—when we started to have to interact with one another to pass—that was when other kids started noticing me. That was when other kids had things to say. And so instead of changing into my gym clothes, instead of partic-ipating, I sat on the bleachers and failed. Every day.

I wasn't the only one sitting out. A few other kids, kids I knew were bullied, too, had their own reasons to sit out. We talked sometimes. But usually we just sat there, watching everyone else interacting, play-ing, having fun. Being themselves. Coming into their own.

Now, I see how calculating I had to be just to look out for myself. Can you imagine going through that for so many years, trying to re-main low-key so that you won't be called out or bullied? Thinking about every single move you make, always adjusting your natural voice and patterns of speech—it was like working overtime all the time. And I was just trying to find myself, like everyone else.

ON THE weekends, Isa and I worked as servers at a restaurant in Span-ish Harlem, where Seli's then-husband, Raul, was part owner. I liked being there, it felt like family. But some of the other employees made me feel the same way that I felt at school, so I held back and didn't let them see the real me.

Luckily, though, I did find my place at the restaurant. Ever since I was young, I've loved to cook. To this day, I find that cooking is a way for me to process and deal with my emotions—it nourishes my body and my soul. For me, cooking is an escape and an outlet for healing from all of the trauma I've experienced in my life. And cooking a meal makes me feel like I've accomplished something productive and good.

In elementary school, I was obsessed with Rachel Ray's show *Thirty-Minute Meals*. Whenever I cooked, whether it was omelets and home fries for breakfast or sandwiches for lunch; I pretended that I was a Food Network star with my own show. I acted like I was on set, talking out loud to the viewers at home, explaining each step. By the time I was working at the restaurant, my brother-in-law knew that I had an interest in cooking, and he asked me if I wanted to help out in the kitchen, to be an assistant chef. Immediately, I said yes.

I loved working with Chef Diego. He was a funny, chubby Mexican guy with a big smile and a kind soul. He was not the judgmental type, and so I never felt unwelcome or uncomfortable around him. He was just cool, always smiling and laughing, always in good spirits. And being able to cook set me free. I was more comfortable in the kitchen with Diego than I was at school, and even though I was there every single day, from three-thirty or four in the afternoon until eleven at night, I never felt burned out or unhappy when I was at work. In fact, it was just the opposite, like my little getaway.

At first, Chef Diego had me prep the ingredients for each dish. Washing, chopping, slicing, mixing—the works. He saw that I was a fast learner, that I'd had experience in the kitchen, and soon, I started taking orders from the floor, making the dishes, and sending them out myself. I had it all memorized: the ingredients, the prep work, the recipes. Once, after having surgery, Chef Diego was out of the restaurant for three weeks. For some reason, the other chef who worked there had just up and left, leaving me as the one in charge. It was the best experience ever. I felt good, confident. *This is for me,* I thought. It was only when I was in the professional kitchen, in charge of the restaurant, that I remembered the aspirations I had when I was a kid, of becoming a chef and having my own show. For the first time in my life, I had a taste of what my future could be.

My brother-in-law would always say to me: "If you're feeling like this is too much with school and everything, just let me know. It's okay if you are—school comes first."

Even though I loved my job, and the confidence it gave me, I was starting to feel drained. I was finding it hard to function at school. Even my teachers were noticing how tired I was all the time. And I didn't want to fail. I wanted to graduate, to go to college, to move on to bigger and better things.

After three months, I made the decision to quit. Working at the restaurant didn't change my experience at school, but it did give me an outlet to express myself. (And, at ten dollars an hour, I felt like I was raking it in!) So when the job was over, I didn't have anything else to distract me from all of the worries, all of the anxieties, all of the calculating that defined my days.

THE ONLY person I really talked to about what I was going through was Kimberly, the girl who lived downstairs. We had that type of relationship where it was just easy to be around one another and open up. She went to a school two stops past mine, so we took the bus and train together every morning and afternoon. And at night, we'd sit on the porch for hours, gossiping and sharing secrets. She told me things about her and her boyfriend that shocked me, but it made me feel comfortable telling her about myself, about how alone I felt at school.

Other times, when I was alone at home, I'd go out onto our roof and watch the sun set behind the Tracey Towers, thinking about my dreams and what I wanted to become, wishing that my life could be different. Wishing that I could be myself 100 percent. I had so many questions about who I was, who I was going to become, that I didn't even know where to start. But there was something about sitting up there—the quiet of it all, the view of this large city all around me—that made me feel better.

I didn't have any words to really describe what I was feeling, but "gay" felt like the closest. For much of my life, people always told me that's what I was. When I denied it to kids at school, they'd just tell me that I was delusional. *Was I?* I tried to think it through: I certainly was attracted to guys—and I'd rather have been one of the girls than be with them. *So, I must be gay, right?* I thought. *I mean, what else could I be?*

Part of me felt like there was still something more to it than that, but I decided that I needed to tell someone, and that someone was Kimberly. I went outside, into the *yardita*, and stepped onto our neighbor's doorstep to see if I could see her inside her living room or dining room. When I spotted her, I knocked on the door, and she and I sat

68

out on the front porch like we always did. Eventually, I mustered up the courage.

"Kimberly?" I said. "I need to tell you something—"

She looked at me. "Yeah?"

"Well—I'm gay."

She smiled. "Jose," she said, "I know!"

She knows? But how?

I wasn't even sure, but it felt good to get it off my chest and confide in someone. I laughed and shrugged. I guessed that if she knew, then it must be true. After this, I felt a little more confident. Maybe I could start showing people the real me.

I STARTED finding people on Myspace who seemed more accepting and more like me than the kids at my school were. And there was one guy I met who stood out from all the others. His name was Jayden. He identified as gay, but he looked kinda hood, like a bad boy. In his profile picture, he wore Pepe jeans and a Sean John shirt. He was my ideal definition of masculinity, and I loved that. There was also something about him that made me feel secure. He wasn't ashamed of who he was, and he was open about his sexuality—even his family knew that we'd been chatting! Once, while we were talking, he put them on the phone. I was flustered and didn't know what to say. I never would have expected them, a Latinx family like my own, to be so comfortable with the whole thing. It got me thinking: *maybe it would be okay if I came out to my family.* But not yet. I was not ready for that yet.

After talking on the phone and video chatting for a few months, Jayden invited me to visit him in Staten Island.

"You mean, skip school?" I asked. The moment I said this, I felt like my heart was up in my throat. I couldn't do something like that!

"We can spend the whole day together," he said.

"Aren't you supposed to be in school?"

"Oh, I'm cutting school."

I thought about this for a bit. Skipping school was not something I wanted to do—but the fact that he was going to do it made me feel a little bolder, like I could do it, too. And I really wanted to see him. On top of this, I dreaded the idea of going to school, hiding the real me, *pretending*, for even one more day.

"Okay," I told him.

The night before, on the porch, I told Kimberly about my plan.

"Are you crazy?" she asked. "Do you even know who he is?"

"Yeah," I said. "Of course I do." The idea that he wasn't who he said he was had crossed my mind, but we had video-chatted, so I knew it was him.

"You sure you wanna go through with this?" she asked, her eyebrows raised in concern.

"Hell yeah," I said.

Chapter 8

MARIZOL & SELENIS

. . . .

That morning, I played it cool. Up at six, out the door by seven. From the outside, nothing was different—I got dressed, ate breakfast, slung my backpack over my shoulder. I acted like today was just any other day. But on the inside, I was all butterflies.

On the subway, Kimberly kept questioning me. "Are you sure you want to do this? Why don't you just go to school?"

"No way," I said. I was going to do this. I had a plan: leave Jayden's by three, be home by six. I tried not to let on how nervous I was, but of course I worried. What if the school called my parents? Would I have to tell them the truth—that instead of going to school, I went all the way to Staten Island to meet up with a guy? I didn't want that day to be the day I came out to my family. I was not ready for that. I wasn't even sure if "gay" fit who I was, but I didn't have any other words to describe what I'd always felt.

Around me, music buzzed from headphones. Businessmen glanced at their watches. Teenagers laughed. I shrank in my seat, trying to avoid being noticed or becoming their target. I couldn't imagine spending another day at school, editing myself, worrying what the other kids would think of me. I needed to get away. I needed to be with someone who accepted me for me. And so when the subway doors opened at

East 180th Street, I stayed in my seat, next to Kimberly, something I'd never done before.

"This is your stop," Kimberly said. "Come on, just go to school."

But I stayed where I was. When the conductor announced the closing of the doors, I took a deep breath and looked out the window as the South Bronx passed by. Two stops later, Kimberly stood up to get off. "Go back to school!" she said. "Oh my God, just turn around and go back!"

"I gotta go," I insisted.

She just shook her head at me, laughing with a smirk. The doors closed, and I was left alone with all my anxieties as the train moved out of the Bronx, under the Harlem River, and down the length of Manhattan. I tried to stay calm.

It wasn't until the subway got to the end of the line that I realized I didn't exactly know how to get to Staten Island. Everyone seemed to be moving in one direction, and I followed the crowd to the dock, to the huge orange ferry floating in the Upper Bay. Out on the water, it was cold and windy. I pulled my hands into the sleeves of my hoodie and went inside. The Statue of Liberty, which I'd never seen in person before, drifted into view. I couldn't believe I was doing this! I felt alive and free, like anything could happen on the other side of the river.

But the closer I got, the more nervous I was. What was he gonna be like in person? Was the school gonna call my parents? I felt like everyone around me knew that I was doing something I shouldn't be doing, like all the adults were eyeing me, wondering why I was going to Staten Island when I should have been at school. I knew I was doing something wrong, but part of it just felt right.

The ferry docked. I made my way down the ramp and saw the bus Jayden had mentioned. Another thirty-minute ride. The bus climbed up into the hills, and I watched as unfamiliar sights passed by: large houses, tall trees, private schools, green lawns. It truly felt like a different world. The bus pulled up to the stop, and I stepped off, and there I saw him, waiting for me. He looked exactly as I pictured: tall, light-skinned, hair pulled back into braids. *Oh my God, he's in front of me!* I told myself to keep breathing.

. . . .

IT WAS LATE afternoon, in the fall of 2006, when I got the call. I was at home, settling into the evening with my then-husband and our three-year-old daughter.

"Jose never went to school today," my sister-in-law Melodie said over the phone.

"What do you mean he never went to school?"

"The neighbor told us Jose skipped school to meet up with a guy he met online."

It was as if I had been kicked in the face. I was dizzy. *Oh my God*, I thought. *We're gonna find him in a ditch.*

I don't remember the drive to Mami and Papi's home in the Bronx. I don't remember what the weather was like, or the traffic, but I'm sure I sped in my little red Subaru.

My mother was in the kitchen, trying to stay busy, but I could tell she'd been crying. My father was pacing around the house. They'd been waiting for me to get there to call the police.

But the dispatcher was dismissive.

"It hasn't been long enough," she said.

I was desperate. "You have to understand: my sixteen-year-old brother went to go meet a *man* he met online."

And those details—sixteen-year-old, man, online—must have sparked some fear in her, too. "We'll send a car over to take down some information."

. . . .

RIGHT AWAY, I realized that Jayden wasn't the kind of guy I thought he was. I knew he was gay, but I imagined him being kind of hood, like the epitome of a straight, masculine guy. A guy who would make me feel truly feminine. But he was feminine like me. And flamboyant as all hell. What was I supposed to do, turn around and go back to school? Hell no! I'd come all the way out here, and I was gonna stick it out. I knew that I liked his personality, that he was nice and accepting. I didn't want to hurt his feelings, so I decided to give it a try.

He gave me a tour of his neighborhood, and we stopped by his school to pick up a copy of his transcript. It felt weird to go to another school on the day I skipped. But his school, like everything else in Staten Island, was different. His classmates seemed friendly—more welcoming and accepting. When he introduced me to his friends, I didn't feel ashamed, or nervous, or afraid to be me. Still, I couldn't help but notice his feminine features, the way he walked.

He took me to his house, and his mom, who was warm and welcoming, offered to make me something to eat. But I was too nervous to want to eat anything. In the middle of the day, we watched a movie and fooled around a little bit. I wasn't into him, but I didn't want to disappoint him or make him think that I was some kind of tease. I'd never kissed anyone before, so of course it was nerve-racking and exciting. But part of me felt like there had to be more to it than that.

I told Jayden that I needed to leave by three to get back to the Bronx by six. "I don't want my parents to worry," I explained.

But I completely lost track of time. We went out to Chinese with his friends, and later, when we were back at his place, I noticed the sky was darkening. I panicked. It was nearly six! We rushed to leave his house and get to the ferry—if I missed it, I'd have to wait a whole hour for the next. But as we were leaving, I noticed a big hickey on my neck.

"Oh my God, what am I gonna do?"

Jayden put a spoon in the freezer for a few minutes and then we rushed to catch the ferry. Thankfully, we made it, and he rode the ferry with me back to the city. His arm was slung around my shoulders, the cold spoon pressed against the place where his mouth had been a few hours before.

My emotions were all over the place. I knew I was going home to some shit, but I didn't know what. Jayden was attentive and comforting, and it was nice to finally feel cared for. I had a really nice day with him, but I also knew that we were just gonna be friends. I didn't tell him that then, though. Instead, I said, "I wouldn't be surprised if they called the cops. I bet sirens are going off outside my house."

· · · ·

I ASKED MY mother, "Was he different this morning?"

"No," she said, her voice cracking. "*Todo normal como siempre.*"

I imagined Jose: baggy jeans and a light-colored polo, several sizes too big, his hair buzzed. I imagined him opening up to someone he didn't know. I imagined Jose being taken advantage of. Raped. His body discarded.

Papi paced around the house, expressing his worry through anger. "Wait till he gets home!"

"Arnol, *por favor,*" my mother said. "*Calmate.*"

I can't believe this is happening, I thought.

"*Le voy a romper la cara!*"

I had wanted to be there for Jose, to support him. But he wasn't out yet, and I didn't want to push him. That night at my parents' house, however, as we were waiting for the cops to arrive, I began to regret this decision. I wished I had been more direct about the dangers being gay could bring—that people have been killed because of their sexual identity, that, as a young person of color, he was vulnerable to being taken advantage of. I wished I had told him that meeting people online was dangerous, that he couldn't just open up to and trust everyone. I wished I had educated him on what it meant to have safe sex. So many thoughts ran through my mind in that moment, and I had already been in enough episodes of *Law and Order* to know that this kind of scenario never ends well.

It's my fault, I thought. *I didn't do enough. And we're going to get that call telling us that his body's been found.*

. . . .

THE SUBWAY pulled into my station and I ran—onto the platform, through the turnstile, down the stairs. My heart was racing. I was sure my family was panicking.

I took the shortcut, and as I rounded the corner of our block, I saw them: cop cars parked along the street, their lights spinning. The front of my house flashed red then blue then red then blue then red then blue. I tried to catch my breath.

What was I going to say? Would I have to tell them I was meeting up with a *guy*? Oh, God. Maybe they'd just be happy that I was home. Maybe they'd just be happy I was safe. Maybe they wouldn't ask too many questions.

. . . .

TWO COPS FINALLY arrived at my parents' house. They didn't want to be there—and they didn't hide the fact that they were annoyed.

One officer sighed. "So, he met a guy online?"

As he said this, I saw the look on his face change ever so slightly. I knew that look. He was judging us, judging Jose for being gay. And that pissed me off.

The other one chimed in: "How do you know it's not someone he knows?"

I was desperate for them to help. "Because my brother doesn't know anyone in Staten Island! He goes to school in the Bronx. He hangs out with a handful of kids in the neighborhood, including the girl downstairs, and she doesn't know who this person is! This is not someone from their normal group!"

Reluctantly, he opened his pad and began to take down some information.

Was there an argument?

Did we think he ran away?

Had he done anything like this before?

No, no, and no.

I heard footsteps coming up the stairs. The door opened, and it was Jose. Alive. And safe.

"Is this him?" the cop asked.

. . . .

OUTSIDE OUR side door, I hesitated. I didn't want to go in. I didn't want to talk about what I'd done that day, or where I'd gone, or who I'd been with. I walked up the steps very slowly, taking my time. Nonchalant-like. I knew I was gonna be in for it.

Inside, everyone was waiting for me: Mami and Papi, Seli, and my sister-in-law. Two cops, their hips wide from their holsters, turned and looked at me when I opened the door. They closed their notebooks, and I pressed myself against the wall so they could get by and leave.

One of them turned to me and said, "Hey, next time, let your family know where you are."

And then the door slammed shut and they were gone. I knew that shit was about to go down.

. . . .

THE OFFICER CLOSED his pad. To Jose he said, "I'm assuming you're all good?"

And after Jose nodded, his eyes cast down at his feet, the two officers brushed past him and left.

The door closed, and there was Jose, standing in the entryway, with a fucking hickey on his neck.

. . . .

THE ENERGY in the room was tense, negative. I had no idea what I was going to say. My mind was blank, but my heart was in my throat.

Papi lunged at me, but Seli stepped in the way. Uh-uh, she shook her head at him.

. . . .

MY FATHER'S ANGER was palpable in that moment. I could feel it radiate off of him.

My sister-in-law stepped back. My father lunged. I stepped in between him and Jose, knowing that he was going to kick Jose's ass if he got ahold of him. I pulled Jose into the dining room, the statue of the saint staring at us, her arms open wide.

"Where were you?"

. . . .

SELI TURNED and looked straight into my eyes. She was not happy. "Where were you?"

I was embarrassed. I worried that everything was about to come out. But then I paused and thought: *Maybe they don't know anything.*

I said the first thing that came to mind: "At the library."

. . . .

WHAT HAPPENED NEXT surprised me. It surprised Jose, and everyone else in the room. It was fast—it was as if my body reacted before my brain could catch up. Before I knew it, redness formed on Jose's face, and he cradled his cheek.

The room went quiet.

How had I, Jose's protector, the one who always made sure that nobody bothered him, that everybody was good to him, lashed out and put my hands on him?

. . . .

I FELT a hard smack across my face. I knew I deserved it. After everything that went down that night, I figured something was going to happen. But I never would have expected for it to be from Seli.

I held my cheek, stinging and raw.

. . . .

"YOU'VE GOT TO be kidding me," I said. "You have got to be kidding me if you think I'm so stupid as to believe your story!"

My sister-in-law broke us apart. "Your brother's on his way and he's pissed."

And this knowledge, that Tito was on his way, immediately snapped me out of my anger.

"Jose," I said. "Come."

I led him to the attic, which had been turned into a studio apartment and had a sturdy lock on the inside. There, I'd be able to talk to him calmly. There, I'd be able to protect him from my brother. And also from my father.

. . . .

SHE TOOK me upstairs, to the attic, the only room with a door that locked. I knew that I needed to tell her about where I was, about what I'd told Kimberly, but it wasn't easy. It was a struggle to get it out. But finally, I told her. Finally, I opened up to her about things I hadn't really talked about with anyone. About Jayden. About being gay. Like Kimberly, she wasn't surprised. I couldn't believe that everyone around me already knew when I wasn't even sure.

. . . .

"WHO DID YOU meet?" I asked. "Who is this person?"

"Some guy I know," he said.

"I thought you met him online."

"Yeah, but it's somebody that I've been talking to." He paused for a moment before saying, "I mean—I'm gay."

"I know," I said.

He giggled and began to smile. "What do you mean?" A look came across his face, a look of both surprise and relief that said, *Finally, I don't have to hide this anymore.*

Whatever anger I had been feeling earlier, it all subsided. Here I was with my baby brother, who was confiding in me, coming out to me after all these years. He trusted me. And I wanted to help him. I remember wanting to hug him hard but feeling like I had to keep my cool, be serious. Now, I regret not following my heart in that moment.

"You're gonna have support," I told him. "I'll always be here."

And then—I don't even know where it came from—before I could think about it, I heard the question come out of my mouth.

"Do you want to be a woman?"

Part II

BEGINNINGS OF A TRANSITION

· · · · · · · · · · · · · · · · · · ·

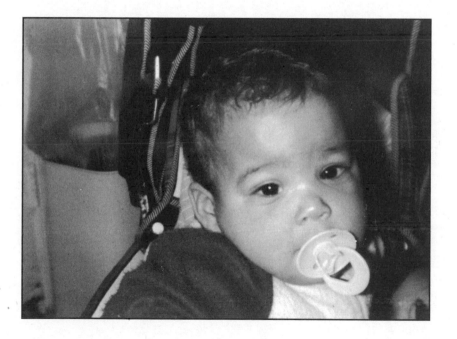

Did I want to be a woman?

I couldn't believe that my sister was asking me that question. What did she even mean by it? *Be a woman.* Was it possible? Did she know something that I didn't?

At this time in my life, I had never heard the term "transgender," nor had I ever met anyone who identified this way. What I had seen on shows like *Jerry Springer* or *Maury* were "transsexuals." And every time, they were portrayed as disgusting freaks. "The Man in the Dress." Or "My Transsexual Love Triangle." Was that how my sister saw me? Is that what she meant when she asked me if I wanted to be a woman?

Because of the body I was born into, I was assigned male at birth. And that assignment, and all of the masculine pronouns that came with it—*he/him/his*—defined everything in my life: my name, my clothes, my toys. It defined how I was supposed to act, how I was supposed to walk, how I was supposed to talk. But my actions, my mannerisms, my interests—my *everything*—were in conflict with what boys were supposed to like and what boys were supposed to do.

When I finally got the courage to come out to the world as gay, I was hesitant. Something about it just didn't fit right. Everyone else around me, though, like Kimberly and my sister, seemed sure. Though it is true that I am and always have been attracted to men, none of us knew the differences between sexual orientation and gender identity. It is different for everyone, but in general, *sexual orientation* refers to who you are romantically, sexually, emotionally, or spiritually attracted to. *Gender identity*, on the other hand, refers to your individual concept of self. Gender identity can mean that you identify yourself as male, as female, as neither, or even as both. The spectrums for sexual orientation and gender identity are infinite, and one person may inhabit multiple identities or orientations throughout their life.

For me, though, I have always identified as female. This was true even when I was a child, when I did not have the language to describe it, and when, later, I had the language but not the courage to live out openly in the world as my true self. Now, because I know the difference between sexual orientation and gender identity, I understand why the label "gay" never quite felt right to me: I was never a male attracted to other males. I am, and always have been, female. The first moment I heard the term "transgender," I grasped it. It was liberating to finally have a way to describe how I'd always felt and to join a community of others like me. Today, I am proud to say that I am trans, but I have also become aware of how labels can confine us and affect others' perceptions of who we are. I am a trans woman, yes. But I am also a complex human being who deserves respect, privacy, and compassion. I am a trans woman, yes. And that does not make my sense of self or my womanhood any less legitimate or real.

All that time I spent alone in my room dressing up in Seli's clothes or putting on makeup or daydreaming about what it would be like to be loved by a boy—those were the moments when I could really just be myself, when I could forget about how other people thought of me (as a boy) simply because of how my body looked when I was born. I thought that my feelings were something shameful, that I would always have to hide. I thought that I could only be my true self alone, behind closed doors.

That night in the attic, when my sister asked me if I wanted to be a woman, my immediate reaction was to say no. I was scared and confused. I didn't want to be thought of as a freak. And I didn't want my family to be ashamed of me.

At the same time, though, that night was the first time I was given permission to even consider separating my sexuality from my gender identity. And it was exciting.

Marizol Leyva

Chapter 9

MARIZOL

. . . .

I never went back to Staten Island after that day with Jayden. We talked on the phone a little bit, and kept somewhat in touch, but I think we both realized that we weren't for each other. It's funny to look back on it now: the two of us were so similar. Extra feminine, both wanting to be with someone more masculine. A couple of years later, I found out that we were even more similar than I could have imagined: we both had embarked on the long, uncertain journey of transitioning.

Still, the experience of going to Staten Island, the mix-up with the police, and the confrontation with my family all made me feel that I could be more open. I knew that I had Seli supporting me, and I became more comfortable putting myself out there. On Myspace, I'd see posters about parties or Kiki Balls, those legendary ballroom-style competitions that combine fashion, performance, and dance, at LGBTQ+ youth centers in the city. Around the time I turned seventeen, in 2007, I started meeting other young people in the community who were just beginning to discover themselves, like me, and we stayed in touch through chat groups and AOL Instant Messenger.

There was this one girl I met on Myspace—Miranda was her name. There was just something about her I found so interesting. For one thing, her fashion was killer. She was small-framed with long brown hair, very well put together, and she had this confidence that just came through. I didn't normally go out of my way to become someone's friend, but I saw that we knew some of the same people, so I sent her a message.

> Hey girl! I think we have some mutual friends in common.
> I just wanna let you know that I really like your style and
> I hope we can meet up one day!!!

To my surprise, she wrote me back right away.

> OMG THANK YOU!!!!!! YOU'RE SO CUTE TOO!!!! YES LETS MEET!

I was smiling mad cheesy. I was so excited that someone like her wanted to be my friend. Soon, we made plans to meet up with a group of others in the Village at this Chinese food place on Christopher Street. I remember feeling, when I got out of the train at West 4th, like I was in a whole new world. Growing up in New York City, I'd always known that the Village was important to the LGBTQ+ community, that it was the site of the Stonewall Riots and essentially the birthplace of the LGBTQ+ rights movement in the United States. But it wasn't until I went there for the first time that I understood what it meant to have a public space feel like home. To this day, getting out at the West 4th station is magical for me. There's something about the energy of the Village that makes you leave all your problems behind. There, I always feel confident and at ease. And that first day, I finally felt free to be myself. Knowing that this was a place where people fought for our rights was liberating, but so was seeing others like me being so free with their body language and dress. Here, no one gave any fucks about what anyone else thought, and when I was there, I felt free to turn it up as much as I wanted. To be whoever I wanted to be.

Like the Stonewall Inn, or the Christopher Street Piers, Golden Woks became a legendary place for the young LGBTQ+ community in New York. It's a place where people go and hang out, pick up some cheap food, and spend time kiking with friends who have become family. Everyone I met seemed to know about the hole-in-the-wall Chinese restaurant just a few blocks from the piers. It's tiny, with only four small tables and a few chairs. It's mostly a take-out place, but whenever we were there, it was always packed. Always a commotion.

That first day I was there, when I met Miranda, we were all crowded around the little tables with our trays of sweet and sour pork and egg rolls that came in a wax-paper bag. Everyone was talking about their sexuality and how they identified, but I was finding it hard to concentrate. The volume of the chatting was super loud, and I got caught up in everything that was happening. I couldn't believe that I was there, with other kids who were like me, and that Miranda was sitting just a few feet away.

Then I heard the reactions.

"What? No way?!"

"Girl, I'da never thought."

"Really?!"

I looked over at Miranda's table, and everyone's face was in shock. I had to know what this was all about.

"What's going on, y'all?"

"Miranda just said she's transgender!"

This was the first time I'd ever heard that word, and I had no idea what it meant.

"Wait—what do you mean? What is that?"

"I'm trans," she said.

I still didn't get it, and so she broke it down in the only way she knew I would understand, though I could tell it made her uncomfortable.

"I used to be a boy," she said quietly. "But I never felt like a boy."

"Oh my God!" I said. "No way!"

But in my mind, I was thinking: *I can't believe it! That's how I've always felt too.*

My brain started spinning, just trying to put things together. I didn't ask her more right then, but that night, when I got home, I started googling every question that came to mind. I learned about what it meant to "transition," or the process of making changes in your life so that your gender expression more fully matches your gender identity. I learned, too, that transitioning can mean many different things, and the decision to transition is very personal and individualized. As a result, one trans person's experience can vary drastically from another's.

And I learned other things. In general, there are two types of transitions: social and medical. *Social transition* refers to decisions such as coming out to friends and family and asking others to use pronouns that match your gender identity. It can include changing your name and adopting new grooming or clothing habits. *Medical transitioning* refers to physical changes you make to your body, usually under the guidance and care of a medical professional. This can involve surgery but also less-invasive medical procedures, such as laser hair removal and hormone therapy. That night, I read about what hormone therapy meant for trans women, how a steady dose of estrogen and testosterone blockers could make your hips rounder, your face softer, your breasts fuller.

I couldn't believe it was real. For so many years, I had imagined an alternate life in which I could live as a girl, and now I knew that I wasn't only dreaming but that it was possible. And I knew someone who'd done it! I didn't know the full details of Miranda's transition at the time, but I saw her living her truth out in the world, her gender expression matching her gender identity.

And if Miranda could transition, why couldn't I? Right away, I felt excited and hopeful—transitioning was something I knew then that I wanted to do. But some of the details scared me. I read about trans men and women being rejected in their communities, trans youth being disowned by their families and becoming homeless. I read about trans girls getting their hormones on the street, with sex work the only way to pay. I read about hormones damaging your liver and bones, about sudden blood clots that could kill you.

I wondered: *Is this sacrifice worth it if I'll finally look how I feel?*

I COULDN'T help but feel like the universe led me to Miranda. I knew there was something special about her when I first saw her Myspace profile, but I didn't know what. After that first day we met in the Village, we became fast friends. She'd spend the night at my house or me at her place. She showed me how she'd make her own clothes, how she'd add studs or bows or rhinestones to jeans and tops, how she'd deconstruct a shirt and put it back together so that it'd hang in a fresh way. She was a few years older than me, and I felt like from her I had so much to learn, but we also had so much in common—growing up, we both felt different from everyone else, like we had to keep everything a secret. She was the first person in my life who I could really talk to, and it was a relief knowing that I wasn't alone.

At the same time, even though I was excited and hopeful to see someone like Miranda fully out there, a part of me was intimidated. It had been a struggle for her at first, but by the time I met her, she didn't have to hide around her family. I wanted to believe that my family would come around, too. But what if I had to choose between them and living my life to its fullest? I was too afraid to confront the possibility.

And then, one day, I received a message from an old friend, a friend who was in a stage of transitioning that was less intimidating to me: Justin, from middle school. Just like people around me had assumed I was gay because of my personality and the way I carried myself, I had made the same assumption about Justin because of how flamboyant he was. But I quickly saw that he had a second profile. In it, Justin was going by the name Melissa and posting pictures in full makeup, in dresses and wigs.

Melissa and I never had the conversation about her identifying as trans, but after meeting Miranda, it was obvious to me. At the time, Melissa would go out in the world as herself. Her parents were not fully accepting of this new identity, so she had to experiment with makeup and clothes behind the closed door of her bedroom. Eventually, her mother came around, realizing that it wasn't just a phase. But her father didn't like it, and even though Melissa was clear with him that she didn't give a damn what he thought, whenever she came home, she toned it down, taking off her wig or changing into more gender-neutral clothes.

I decided to cut school and meet up with her. She showed me her collection of makeup and wigs, how she'd take photos of herself with her webcam. We hit up the shops along Jerome Avenue. Rainbow, Foot Locker, the accessories store next to the nail salon. It was there that I found my wig: long and dark brown with a straight bang. London Girl, it was called. It made me feel truly feminine, like I could pass.

Back at her house, Melissa helped me get all done up and set up a box fan so that my hair could blow in the wind. I remember the feeling of butterflies when I saw the pictures. It wasn't much, but I got a small idea of what it would be like to live another kind of life.

"You've gotta come up with a name," she said to me.

I used to daydream about what my name could be if it could be different. I wanted something Spanish, something that represented me. And out of nowhere, it came to me: Marizol. I didn't know anyone with the name, and I wanted to know the meaning. We looked it up—"ocean" and "sun"—and right away, I knew it was me.

I WASN'T ready to wear feminine clothes in public, but with my new Myspace profile, my friends in the community started calling me Mari. On the weekends, I'd go to the Village to meet up with Miranda and the others. There was a group of us who'd always get together, meeting up at Golden Woks or the pizza shop or the big church on 6th Avenue. We became a little entourage and started calling ourselves the Crazy Eights, even though our number was constantly changing. We stopped by tattoo parlors, dreaming about the tattoos or piercings we'd someday get. We window-shopped for costumes and wigs. We went to parties and Kiki Balls hosted at LGBTQ+ centers around the city, always looking put together and fly. We each had our own fashion sense, but somehow our individual styles always complemented each other's. People started noticing us, wanting to hang out with us. And our group got bigger and bigger.

Lorenzo was one of the core members of the Crazy Eights, and one of my closest friends. He was a short guy, half Dominican and half Puerto Rican, and had skin that seemed to glow. He was always smiling. He was quirky and fun, with a sharp, sarcastic sense of humor. But more than this, Lorenzo was a good, sweet guy. He never wanted to be part of any drama, and he always gave me good advice. And even though I never talked to him about transitioning, he'd always tell me that he'd support me if I wanted to do it.

It was so nice to finally feel like part of a community that supported and loved me. So many people in the LGBTQ+ community are shunned or disowned by their families because of their sexual or gender identity, so they have to create a new family, a family of people like them. I was grateful to have these friends in my life. Every time we met up, it was like an escape from all that we were dealing with at home or at school. We could open up to one another about these sensitive, personal struggles. And we could laugh and feel comfortable and just have the time of our lives, without having to worry about what anyone else would think or say or do.

OF ALL of the parties and events, the Kiki Balls were my favorite. They were always hot and mad crowded. I loved being there, feeling the excitement heat up the room. I gravitated toward the trans girls, watching them vogue and dance and display nothing but confidence as they walked categories like Face or Femme Queen Realness. You have to be bold to get up there and show everyone who you are, and these women were confident, beautiful, and free. *Damn*, I'd think. *I wanna be just like that.* But I didn't know if I had it in me. Mostly, I was worried about how my family would react. Still, I was always amazed how, at these little balls, you could feel validated. How you could feel like somebody.

For the category of Face, everything has to be proportioned. Your bone structure. Your eyebrows. Your teeth. Your smile has to be perfect. Your skin has to be baby-soft. One night, my crew and I were at a Kiki Ball at the LGBTQ+ center at 149th Street in the Bronx. We saw that Clarissa was there, from the House of Milan. Clarissa was born to walk Face, and everyone was telling me that I should battle her.

"No way!" I said. "She's so beautiful."

Miranda smiled at me. "Mari, so are you!"

"You are the only one who can go up against her!" Lorenzo insisted.

Maybe I could beat her, I thought. I knew Clarissa was more experienced, but I was young and baby-faced and had recently had my eyebrows done. I was looking fly in a purple shirt and a purple sweater, with name-plate jewelry: chain, earrings, and ring. I decided to just go for it and walk the way I was, without any makeup or alterations.

"Okay, I'll take it home for us," I said.

The music for Face began to play, and when I heard the beat, my heart started racing.

"Lorenzo, what am I gonna do?"

"Just sell it!"

The crowd started clapping and chanting.

And then the emcee called out, "Face Category, come through!"

There were six of us in total, and we walked down the aisle, two-by-two. The crowd was on both sides, cheering and chanting, but I tried to ignore everything around me and just work it. I touched my face. I lifted my chin to show off my bone structure. I looked up high above the crowd. I got a rush from putting myself out there, from doing something I'd never done before. The whole time, I was thinking to myself, *I can't believe I'm doing this!*

The judges touched my face to test for smoothness. When it was time for scoring, they lifted their fingers: ten, ten, ten, ten. I was on to the second round, and then the next. Before I knew it, it was time for me to go up against Clarissa, one-on-one.

I got really nervous. Before the final round began, I said to my friends, "Y'all made me do this—you better be going crazy!" They moved to the front of the room, near the judges' table, right beside the House of Milan. It was a real battle, what everyone had been waiting for, and the chants shook the house.

Crazy Eights!

Milan!

Crazy Eights!

Milan!

To win Face, you have to keep your face serious and stern. You have to let your expression say, "I'm the shit, and I know it!" During that battle against Clarissa, I let myself get distracted by the crowd. I became more timid. In the end, Clarissa won the grand prize, but I wasn't bothered by that. I had done something new. I had put myself out there. I was starting to find myself.

WE DIDN'T have any LGBTQ+ parties or Kiki Balls in my neighborhood in the Bronx. In general, the nightlife in the area was kinda sad. El Coral could be poppin' on some nights, like when they'd have a live band or a DJ spinning, but not that many people would come out. Somehow, I got the idea that I could throw a party for us and make it happen.

Paul was the name of the promoter at El Coral, and he was always outside on his phone, doing business. We first met when I was planning my sixteenth birthday, and afterward, whenever I'd walk by, he'd say to me, "Hey, you've gotta come check us out!"

Of course, he talked like this to everyone to get lots of people to come to the club, but I liked the attention I got from him. He was tall, probably six-foot-three, with curly hair that was shaped up nice. He dressed very Dominican: buttoned-up shirt, a good belt, pointy shoes, tight pants.

"Okay, cool, cool!" I would say.

One day, I finally said to Paul, "Yo, why don't you let me throw a party for my people? I can definitely bring some people out."

When he agreed, I told him that he needed to have karaoke and that we needed to make the little area by the bar more of a club where people would wanna hang out. I started promoting the party on Myspace, telling my friends on AIM, everybody I knew from the LGBTQ+ centers, the Kiki Balls to come. Friends of mine, and even people I didn't know, commented on the bottom of the flyer, tagging others and saying that they'd be there.

The night of the party was poppin'. El Coral was totally packed, with a line wrapped around the corner outside. After we reached capacity, people started to come through the fire exit to get inside.

Paul looked at me in disbelief. "I did not expect this!"

And, shit, neither did I! I thought about my sixteenth birthday party, how no one showed. How I had hoped for something like this—a crowded dance floor, people celebrating and having a good time. But unlike at my birthday party, that night at El Coral I felt proud: this was the first LGBTQ+ party in my neighborhood, and it happened because of *me*. People who lived nearby looked out their windows at the crowd, wondering where all these people had come from. After a short time, the party started to look like a ball, with people dancing, voguing, going off!

"Oh my God," Paul stood off to the side, laughing. "You guys are insane!"

Even some of my family came. Tito, Tony, and Isa all stopped by, and a few hours in, when I was all hot and sweaty from running around and hosting, making sure that my friends were having a good time, Seli showed, too. I'd always loved my sister's fashion, and I was excited to show her off. That night, she wore a sequined halter top that I adored, tight jeans, a silver belt, and some high-heeled sandals. Her hair was pulled back, with a small rose tucked behind her ear.

Seli and I took a seat at the bar, both amazed at all the people who were there, buying drinks and dancing.

"Can you get me a drink or something?" I asked her. I was only seventeen and had never had a drink before, but this felt like a special night.

"Uh, no."

"Oh come on! Get me one of those drinks that comes in a martini glass."

She laughed and ordered two cosmos.

It was the first time my sister and I were out together at a bar, enjoying each other's company and all the commotion around us. I was proud to have her see how happy and comfortable I was with my people—and I was proud for my people to see me with her! I'll never forget the feeling I had that night with my sister, drinking that pink drink in a fancy glass, surrounded by my community: I felt fabulous.

I then noticed a guy—a cute guy, who looked a bit like Usher—looking at me.

"Um, do you see that guy over there?"

Seli turned and looked.

"He keeps looking at me! What the hell?"

She smiled. "He's kinda cute.

"Yeah, right? He is kinda cute."

I remember being surprised by myself in that moment. This was the first time after that night in the attic that I was open with my sister in such a way. It was also the first time I noticed that a guy was checking me out, and it was exciting. I looked at him, and then I looked away, and then I was mad giggly.

A few minutes later, when Seli got up to go to the bathroom, he walked up to me.

"Hey, how you doing?" He put out his hand and said, "I'm Nathaniel."

"Oh, hi," I said. "I'm good."

We started talking, flirting like crazy. By the end of the night, we had exchanged numbers. It wouldn't be the last time I saw him.

I WAS happy. I was becoming more and more comfortable being me, especially when I was with my people. Finally, I could be the open, energetic, fun person I always wanted to be. But in the back of my mind, I still thought about what it would be like to live my life fully as Marizol.

I talked to Miranda about transitioning, and she was nothing but supportive. She'd say, "If you really feel that way, do it!"

Or, "I can tell that you really want to."

Or, "I think you should do it, but I think you're just having a hard time accepting yourself."

It was true. But more than that, I was worried about what my family would think. I never told anyone other than Miranda about wanting to transition, and she listened, like a real friend. And then she talked to me about what it was like for her and how she eventually got her family to understand and accept where she was coming from. Miranda not only showed me that my dreams were in fact possible, but she also reminded me that I deserved to live my truth.

Maybe I could do that, I began to think. *Maybe I could actually take the steps Miranda took. Maybe I could transition, too.*

Chapter 10

SELENIS

. . . .

I was not okay with Jose skipping school. And though I knew that he was meeting other young people in his community online, I was not comfortable with it. That night in the attic after the Staten Island incident, I said to him, "I want you to be who you need to be. But you cannot be putting yourself in danger." The internet, chat rooms—it was all new at that time, and I became obsessed with reading harrowing stories about cyber-predators, about young people who ended up missing—or worse—after meeting a stranger. I was terrified, and even more so after learning that being gay put Jose in even more jeopardy. I needed him to realize the dangers of what he might be walking into when he went to meet up with someone he thought was his age, alone, all the way across the city.

I reached out to an NYPD precinct in the South Bronx near Jose's school and was connected with a female detective in the Special Victims Unit, Detective Flores. I explained to her why I was reaching out, what I feared could have happened to Jose, the fact that I needed my baby brother to be safe. She was immediately understanding. "Just bring him in," she said. What a difference from those judgmental cops who responded to our call that night.

The day of the meeting, Jose was cranky and annoyed.

"Do we have to do this?" he asked in the car on the way there.

"YES!" I said. "Yes, we have to!"

In person, Detective Flores was friendly but very businesslike. She had a masculine presence—from her husky build and short brown hair to the man's-style pantsuit she wore. She introduced us to her partner, a white detective, and the four of us went into an interrogation room. We walked through the busy precinct where detectives and officers bent over paperwork, made calls, went about their jobs. No one seemed to look at us twice or show us any concern except for Detective Flores.

The interrogation room was bare, with two metal chairs, a metal table, and a single light hanging overhead. It looked exactly like the sets of *Law and Order* I was used to working on. It was dreary and cold, not a happy place at all. Jose took a seat, and Detective Flores sat across from him. Her partner stood by, but I got the feeling that he wasn't terribly interested in sticking around for the lecture that was to come. I felt like we were on one of those boot camp TV specials, scaring Jose into a saintlike life by showing him gory photographs of murder victims or how one bad decision could lead to irreparable consequences. But I didn't care. I felt like this was the only way I could get through to him.

Detective Flores started to explain to Jose the danger he could have gotten himself into that day, breaking it down into specific cases the precinct had seen. She was direct and to the point, telling him about scenarios of teenagers encountering friends or love interests online, going to meet them, and then ending up missing. Every time it was always the same: teens thought they were meeting someone their age, but when they showed up, their "friend" or "boyfriend" or "girlfriend" ended up being a man twice their age. A man with a criminal record. A man who was a registered sex offender. And then came the stuff of nightmares: rapes, murders, bodies in ditches. Kids who had been bullied at school, who were questioning themselves in some way, or who felt isolated or out of place were especially vulnerable to this kind of manipulation.

"It doesn't usually end well, like your situation did," she said.

And then she loosened up a little. She had a tough exterior, but through it I started to see genuine concern for Jose.

"Look," she said. "You have to be extra careful. People like *us*, we have got to be really careful. Especially online."

When she said this—"people like *us*"—I didn't think she meant those who identify as Latinx. I think she meant those who identify as LGBTQ+. In that moment, I felt like an outsider, watching this woman trying to have a real connection with Jose. It was so much more than just cop to young man—it was her saying, *I care about you, not because it is my job to but because we belong to the same tribe.*

After that, there wasn't much else left for her to say. I thanked her and her partner, who was finally relieved of his duty witnessing this interaction, and then Jose and I left.

At the time, of course, I knew nothing of the broader dangers that LGBTQ+ individuals face, like homelessness or participation in sex work. I didn't know how vulnerable Jose would be to all kinds of predatory violence. And I had no way of even considering the issues that plague LGBTQ+ youth on the internet today, like cyberbullying, online harassment, and threats or how these particular types of violence can lead to depression, post-traumatic stress disorder (PTSD), self-harm, and even suicide. And yet, despite these dangers, for many LGBTQ+ youth, the resources and community available online can be lifesaving. It can be their only opportunity to learn that there are other people in the world like them and that things can get better. But that day, I was in full-on protection mode, wanting to do all I could to make sure that Jose was safe.

You see?! I wanted to say on the drive back to my parents' house. *You can't do this!*

But I stayed quiet in the car, letting him process all that had been presented to him.

AROUND THIS TIME, my life had begun to fall apart. My career wasn't going anywhere, and financially, I wasn't doing well. On top of that, my husband and I were more roommates than we were a married couple. We were functional, but cracks had begun to form, cracks that quickly made their way to the foundation of our marriage. We'd have one good day followed by a horrible week. Then repeat. I was miserable. I tried to keep things to myself, but my parents knew. They could see those cracks in my marriage well before I could. And when our landlord told us that she was going through a divorce and needed her apartment back, my parents offered us the attic apartment in their home, the same attic where I'd had the instinct to ask Jose if he wanted to be a woman.

The apartment in my parents' attic was not a place I would have normally felt comfortable living in. It was a studio, with very low ceilings, a tiny bathroom, and a little kitchen with barely enough space for a table and chairs. In the bedroom area, we could fit a dresser, a little bed for my daughter, who was nearing four around this time, and our bed. And the fact that I was back at my parents' house made me feel like such a loser. But, at the same time, it was comforting to be there. To be home, and to be near Mami and Papi. My mother helped care for Alina, and my husband and I could make what little money was coming in stretch further.

Even though I was living in the same house as Jose, I didn't see him all that much. A distance formed between us, and soon, I started to see a change in him. I didn't know what was going on in his life exactly, but I did know that he was partying all the time. He broke curfew, coming home at two or three in the morning, totally trashed. My mother found a stash of women's clothes in a backpack in the basement that she knew belonged to him, but we didn't know where he was going or what kind of trouble he was getting himself into. Our don't-ask, don't-tell situation was getting harder and harder to maintain.

In the mornings, Mami tried to get him up for school.

"Jose," she'd say, knocking on his door. "*Es hora de levantarte!*"

But he didn't go to school. Instead, he slept until four in the afternoon and then went out partying again. My parents were at a loss for what to do. Papi even threatened to remove Jose's bedroom door from the hinges.

Another time, he brought Jose a suitcase. "If you're not going to school, then you can get your stuff and get out!"

And then one day, my parents received their monthly bank statement and saw that something was very, very wrong. Mami and Papi were meticulous with their spending, and so the fact that a large sum of money—nearly $18,000—had just gone missing was incredibly disconcerting. Papi went to the bank and filed a report saying that the money had been stolen.

What the hell was happening to our family? I thought. But I wasn't able to help. I was treading water, barely keeping my head above the mess that was becoming my life. I had struggled with depression in the past, and it continues to be something I battle to this day, but growing up, it was never something I felt comfortable discussing or sharing with others. Unfortunately, this is the way it is in many communities: shame surrounds mental illness, and a constant fear of being judged or stigmatized by others makes it difficult for individuals to seek help, whether through therapy or medication.

At this time in my life, I didn't have the knowledge or resources I have today, and my depression took a sharp turn. I started thinking about how I could just escape from it all, how I could get into my car and drive it straight off the George Washington Bridge. As a mother, it is hard for me to admit these things. The feeling that you could abandon your child—I have never felt so guilty as I did during that time. I would think about leaving, about how I could die, and then I would see my daughter's face, and she would smile at me and everything would come tumbling down at once. *How could I leave her, this sweet, innocent child? Who would be there for her?* I have always loved Alina more than anything, and I knew that I couldn't do that to her. But the fact that I considered it made me feel worse. *If I can think of abandoning everything*, I'd think, *I must be a really bad person.*

It is exhausting to fall into these kinds of cycles. It is impossible to think clearly, to have the mental capacity to piece things together that, in retrospect, were so overwhelmingly obvious.

Chapter 11

MARIZOL

. . . .

I knew where Mami kept her ATM card: in the top drawer of her dresser. One day, a voice entered my head and refused to leave, no matter how much I tried to shut it out. *Take the money. Go drink, go shopping, use it to pay for your transition.* I never wanted to hurt my family or to betray their trust. But something snapped inside of me. Eventually, I gave in to its demands.

That first time, I waited until late at night to get the card. It was kept in a paper sleeve, and inside was a little slip with the PIN. I walked down the hill to the bank. I tried not to think about what I was doing. I took the card out of the sleeve and slid it into the reader on the door to get into the room with the ATM. I put the card into the machine, reread the PIN, and punched it in.

Now, I wonder how I could have done such a thing to the people who loved me most. It all happened so quickly that it is difficult to put the pieces back together and re-create what led up to that dark point. Though I was finding myself, though I was having positive experiences that would shape the rest of my life, I was also, at the same time, looking for ways to cover up years of pain and secrets. I thought I was in control, but small, seemingly insignificant decisions quickly snowballed into consequences that were too much for a seventeen-year-old to handle.

ONE DAY, with Melissa, I decided to finally go to the Village dressed not as Jose but as Marizol.

Seli had moved into the attic apartment in my parents' house with her husband and daughter. I didn't know exactly what was going on with her, but I could tell by her energy things weren't totally right. When she was out of the house, I snuck some dark jeans from her closet. But I needed a top, shoes, some accessories. Melissa and I went to our shops on Jerome Avenue, looking for the perfect outfit. I found a black and white top and these cute black flats with a little gray on the toe. They didn't have my size at Rainbow, so I had to squeeze into a pair a half size too small.

We got ready at Jackie's house. She was a girl Melissa and I knew from middle school, someone with whom we didn't have to hide or feel ashamed. Right away, after telling her about Marizol and showing her my page, she started to refer to me with feminine pronouns (*she/her/hers*). She said to me, "Oh my God, this *is* you!" Over the next several years, our relationship would be full of highs and lows. We would argue like cats and dogs, with loud fights that sometimes turned physical. But I always felt accepted by her. Like I could just be. That day, I wore my London Girl wig and some of those nineties-style gold bamboo hoops. I didn't have much makeup on, just some lipstick, mascara, and blush.

"Oh my God, girl!" Melissa said to me. "You look so good!"

"Really?" I asked. My feet were killing me.

Now, looking back, I see how Melissa was giving me a push to put myself out there. She was used to doing this, dressing as a woman in public. She was comfortable and confident, a big personality who always looked good. I was so nervous when we walked through my neighborhood to the train; I was scared that someone would recognize me, that someone would call me out as a man dressed in women's clothes. But not Melissa. That day, guys were tryna holla her on the train. And there I was, the ugly duckling with some red-ass cheeks, sitting quietly while I watched her flirt with boys who didn't know who she was.

The closer we got to the West 4th stop, however, the more at ease I felt. And when we exited the station, the uplifting energy of the Village gave me the confidence boost I needed. Later, we went to a Kiki Ball, and when we walked in everyone was asking: "Who's the new girl?"

It was exciting.

IT WAS around this time that I started seeing my first boyfriend: Nathaniel, the guy I'd met while throwing the party at El Coral. He was older than me and had a good job in engineering, so we didn't see each other all that much. But we talked on the phone and sent each other texts all the time.

"Hey, I miss you. I want to see you," I'd tell him.

And he would come and pick me up in his car, and we'd drive around or just sit in his car parked outside of my house and talk or go back to his place to watch movies and eat takeout on the couch. He had come out not too long before that party at El Coral, so he wasn't all that comfortable being affectionate in public. On the train, he'd sit far away from me so that people wouldn't know we were together. But I felt safe with him. Comfortable being myself. He genuinely cared about me and wanted me to make good choices, to do something good with my life. He believed that I had good things ahead of me. And he made me feel special. The way he spoke to me made me feel all giggly and warm, like I was the only person in the world. I didn't tell him much about my friends in the community or how I was thinking about transitioning, but he made me happy. I felt like a girl who had a boyfriend for the first time.

One night, he cooked me dinner, and I remember feeling so cared for, like he was trying to do something special for me. Later, when we said goodbye at the end of the night, he said to me: "Be careful. I love you."

I was flying.

FOR THE first time in my life, I was feeling confident. I was starting to embrace who I was, if only around a few select people, and I wanted to celebrate being me.

And because we were teenagers, celebrating me meant experimenting, trying new things—and breaking the rules. It was in the legendary Oval Park that I had my first blunt and drank my first beer. I was with Jackie and a couple of her friends. We sat down on benches not too far from my house. I was nervous that someone was going to catch us. My brothers always hung out in the park. What if they showed up to play basketball? Or what if one of their friends playing basketball saw us and said something?

"They can see us here!" I said.

"No way," Jackie said. "We're covered by the trees."

But I knew that was not the case. If I was sitting in my room, or in Mami and Papi's room, looking out onto the park, this spot was visible from the window.

"Mari, get over it! It's not that big of a deal."

"No, we gotta move," I insisted.

They rolled their eyes but humored me, and we moved to another set of benches in an area that was more hidden.

Jackie passed the blunt to me, and I took a hit. It burned the back of my throat, and I started coughing like crazy. Then she handed me the forty, and I took a long drink. I thought to myself, *Okay, this I can handle*. Pretty soon, I started to feel a little woozy. A little cute. A little less insecure or worried or self-conscious.

On Halloween, we went to the parade, and I dressed as Marizol. I loved it all—the costumes, the colors, how everyone was celebrating and dancing and free. Afterward, we hung out at the Christopher Street Pier until four in the morning, the music blasting. We vogued and danced and cheered each other on. For us, it was a place of freedom and laughter where we could be ourselves. At school and with my family, I was still tryna lay low, to not attract so much attention. I hated feeling like I had to hide, knowing that a whole other world existed for people like me.

BY THIS time, my sophomore year, I wasn't really being bullied much at school. It took me a while to open up to other kids, and I was still pretty shy, but there was this one kid, Timothy, who I felt more comfortable with. He wasn't out, but everyone got the sense that he was gay. He was a year above me and friends with all the dancers, the popular girls. I started to get to know him and the people he was friends with, and I felt a little less lonely. Soon, I felt close enough to him to open up a little, to tell him about how Melissa and I would dress up and do photo shoots. Close enough to show him Marizol's Myspace page.

That was a mistake.

He put me on blast. He showed all the cool girls Marizol's Myspace. And they showed the jocks. Soon, the football players in class were asking me, "Hey, Jose—who's Marizol?" And once again came the teasing. The names. I had been doing well in school. I had plans of graduating, of going to college, of leaving the neighborhood and fully living my life as me—as Marizol. I wanted to go places. To be somebody. My brothers hadn't graduated, and they were always telling me, "Finish school." Or, "Get good grades." I wasn't a straight-A student or anything, but for the most part, I tried to do well in my classes. But this bullying began to wear me down. Everyone else seemed comfortable and free to be themselves, not scared of being around groups of kids.

I didn't tell anyone at home what was going on. I pretended that I had friends, that everything was going fine. I couldn't go to Seli with my problems because she didn't even know about Marizol. But it got so bad at school that I stopped going to lunch altogether.

My teachers knew I was being bullied. Just like in middle school, they stood by and watched how the other kids treated me. Some of them would even say to me things like, "If you toned it down a little bit, you wouldn't be such a target." Back then, in the mid-two-thousands, I didn't know of any support for LGBTQ+ youth in schools in the Bronx. There may have been city- or nationwide initiatives, but it was not something that was discussed at any of the schools I attended or any of the schools my friends attended. And now, though there might be greater tolerance, awareness, and support in schools like the ones I went to, LGBTQ+ kids are still targets. They are more than twice as likely as non-LGBTQ+ youth to experience verbal harassment and bullying,[1] which leads to greater rates of self-harm. Lesbian, gay, and bisexual youth are almost five times as likely to have attempted suicide than heterosexual youth,[2] and nearly half of transgender individuals have attempted suicide at some point in their lives.[3]

I felt only one teacher of mine was understanding and cared about me—Miss Greene, my social studies teacher.

"Look," she said to me one day, "why don't you just come and eat lunch in my classroom?"

"Really?"

"Yeah, why not?"

And so during my lunch hour, I'd go get my food from the cafeteria, try to avoid all the stares and whispers in the lunch line, and go back to her room. She sat at her desk, doing her computer work, and I was off to the side at a student desk, eating my lunch quietly and doing my homework.

WHEN I was out with my friends, I could forget about what was happening at school. Jackie and I started partying a lot, usually with Miranda and others from our little entourage. I started dressing as Marizol when we went out—to house parties, to El Coral, to LGBTQ+ clubs in Manhattan or Brooklyn or the Bronx. I had a stash of clothes and wigs and shoes that I kept in the basement in a spare room, where I hoped nobody would find it.

One night I decided to get ready at home instead of at Jackie's. It was just getting dark, which meant I had to walk out in the open as Marizol to get to Jackie's place, where we'd pregame until late into the night before going out. I was supposed to be home by midnight, but by this point in my life, I never followed curfew. The parties didn't even get poppin' until one in the morning! That evening, I put on my London Girl wig, some makeup, tight jeans. I wore pointy-toed boots and carried a big purse. When I left our house, I put my head up high, and I kept it there as I walked down the hill, past the bus stop and Mami's nail salon and the deli I went to every day in middle school for a bacon-egg-and-cheese with salt, pepper, and ketchup. A group of people turned the corner and I realized that church had just let out and that Mami would be on her way home. And that's when I saw her.

I didn't know whether I should duck into the deli and hide or turn around the block and avoid her altogether. I panicked, but I was running out of time. With every passing second, she and I were getting closer and closer to one another. Finally, I had no choice but to look straight ahead and walk past her like I was just any other person. I took a deep breath and went for it.

And just like that, she walked past me and it was over.

Did she not recognize me?

I turned around to see if she was gonna do a double take. She didn't. I couldn't believe it!

I was relieved she didn't catch me, of course. But I was also happy, excited, that my own mother didn't recognize me. *Maybe I could pass for real all the time,* I thought.

EVEN THOUGH I didn't feel like I could be fully out there with my family, I started to push the limits more and more. I wore magnetic earrings. Tight clothes that showed off my figure.

Papi wasn't happy about it.

"Jose," he said, "why do you have to be so feminine?"

"What do you mean?"

"I mean, you can be gay, but do you have to be so flamboyant about it?"

I rolled my eyes. *Papi, you have no idea,* I thought. If it had been up to me, I would've had my hair done, my nails done, the whole nine. I would've worn a bra! This was nothing.

"This is who I am!" I said. "Can't you just leave me alone?"

"Take it off, Jose," he insisted.

"No! This is me!" I went into my room and slammed the door shut.

I was angry. At him for wanting me to tone it down. At the world for not letting me just be myself. Even at home, I felt like I didn't really fit in. Isa had been adopted by Mami and Papi when she was four, which meant that she could legally use the Leyva name as her own.

The process of my adoption never went through, so I was stuck with my birth father's name. I resented not officially being a part of the family like Isa was. And I was angry at Jose Sr. for not signing over his rights. On top of this, memories from that time I spent at my biological parents' house kept coming up—memories that continue to haunt me to this day.

I STARTED partying so hard and staying out so late that I couldn't get up and get to class on time. It was hard being in school knowing about this whole other world where people like me were not only accepted but also celebrated. I would fantasize about what it would be like to show up one morning as Marizol and say, "I am here! This is me!"

But ideas like these, even when they were exciting, made me panic. What would my principal say? Would I get sent home? What would the other kids do to me? My mind flooded with memories of being bullied in elementary and middle school. Of being called faggot. Of being shunned and having no friends. Of being lonely. I always pretended it didn't bother me, like I didn't give a fuck, but of course it hurt. Of course it made me afraid to really open up.

I wished I could just be like everyone else. That I could go to prom, in a gown, with my boyfriend. That I could graduate. But it seemed like I had to choose between having those experiences and being myself. I was falling into a dark place. I'd think, *Nobody can hear me, so I'm just gonna make noise.* I knew that I couldn't be myself and keep going to school, so I partied. And the more I kept doing things I knew I shouldn't be doing, the more that voice inside my head said, *Fuck it. Enough is enough.* But I wasn't bold enough to say it out loud, so I spoke through my actions.

I wasn't eighteen yet. To officially drop out, a parent had to go to the school office and sign a form. Papi was furious. One morning, when I should have been at school but instead was hungover and trying to sleep it off, he brought me some luggage and yelled, "If you're not gonna go to school, then you can pack your things and leave." But I couldn't imagine going to school—a place I was always hiding—for even just one more day. I promised Mami I would get my GED instead. She finally relented and agreed to sign the form to get me out of school.

When Mami and I got to the school, I started to question my decision. I knew that I shouldn't do it. But at the same time, I knew that I couldn't just keep going back, pretending to be somebody I wasn't. In the office, the counselor slid us the papers.

Maybe I could still stick it out, I thought. *I can still graduate and make something out of myself.*

But then I asked myself: *Am I going to live for myself or for everyone else?*

I signed the papers and so did Mami. I was out of school for good.

Now, looking back, I think that if I hadn't skipped school to meet with Jayden that day in Staten Island, if I hadn't had to come out to my family, if I hadn't met Miranda and known that transitioning was in fact possible—if none of those things had happened, I think I would have stuck it out and graduated. But that would have meant hiding who I was for who knows how much longer, and once I began to learn who I was, I couldn't go back. I made the decision not to hide.

But now I know that I *was* still hiding. I was hiding my true self from Mami and Papi and the rest of the family. All of the partying, which started as a celebration, quickly became a crutch. A way for me to hide from my feelings, from my inability to always and fully be the real me.

The thing about partying is that it costs money, and I had none. My friends would be generous sometimes, sharing liquor and whatnot, but I could sense that their generosity was running out. And without them, without the partying to forget my demons, I was going to have to face them head-on. And I wasn't ready for that.

When I first withdrew Mami and Papi's money from the ATM, I realized I liked being the one buying everyone drinks. Supplying the party, I felt, once again, like I was being celebrated and loved. Of course, it wasn't a full, unconditional love—deep down, I knew my friends were using me—but during the party, it felt like acceptance nonetheless. It was only when the party was over, or when I woke up the next day, hungover and sick, that all of those emotions, all of those insecurities, all of those memories would get the better of me. And so I kept the party going for as long as I could, using Mami's ATM card to withdraw more and more and more.

ONE NIGHT, I came home really late, maybe around two o'clock, trashed. Mami and Papi were asleep, but Seli was there, waiting.

"What do you think you're doing, Jose?"

I didn't respond. The room was spinning. I was gonna be sick.

"You're only seventeen years old!" she yelled. "You have to stop this! It's out of control!"

I ran to the bathroom and bent over the toilet, heaving. She was right, of course. It was getting out of control, but she didn't even know the half of it. After I was finished, I couldn't help but cry.

"I'm such a bad person," I said.

"Jose, you have to stop the partying. You think your friends are your friends, but they're not."

Mami said this to me all the time—"*Esos no son amigos!*"—but it would take much worse for me to really understand what she meant by it.

Chapter 12

SELENIS

· · · · · · · · · · ·

I was disappointed to learn that Jose was dropping out of school, but I wasn't surprised. It was easy to see that something of that nature was going to happen. He was spending more time not going to school than going to school, and though we didn't talk about it at all, I imagined that school was difficult for him socially. I knew that bullying was something he had encountered from a very young age, and I assumed it was something that hadn't just gone away.

Now, we know so much more about LGBTQ+ youth being mistreated at school than we did back then. LGBTQ+ students are more at risk of being picked on or assaulted by their peers, but these are not the only factors that contribute to hostile learning environments. A recent report by the Gay, Lesbian & Straight Education Network (GLSEN) called *Educational Exclusion: Drop Out, Push Out, and the School-to-Prison Pipeline among LGBTQ Youth* describes how LGBTQ+ youth may be more likely to be disciplined by school officials.[4] These discriminatory practices and policies can cause LGBTQ+ students to feel unsafe or uncomfortable in school, and this lack of safety or comfort can lead to poorer academic performance, higher dropout rates, and potential involvement in the criminal justice system. These realities are even harsher for LGBTQ+ students of color, even in predominantly Black and Latinx schools. I can only imagine how difficult it was for Jose at that time; it's no wonder that he wanted out.

Jose had made a deal with my mother, promising that he would get his GED, but I was skeptical. Not that he wasn't capable; it just didn't seem like Jose was in a place in his life where he could be terribly proactive. But I was caught up in my own struggles at the time, and there wasn't anything I could do about it other than hope that he would follow through, that he would get his GED and start working and supporting himself, because I couldn't deal with anything else on top of the chaos in my own life.

WHEN MY FATHER returned from the bank after filing a report about the money that had been stolen, he brought home some difficult information. The money had been withdrawn on numerous occasions with my mother's ATM card.

"I tried to explain to them that you never use your ATM card," Papi said. "And they asked if maybe the card had been stolen."

"*No, yo tengo la tarjeta,*" Mami said, rushing to her bedroom.

My mother never used her ATM card—she didn't really know how to use an ATM card, to be honest, and she kept it in the top drawer of her dresser, under her underwear and socks, with the PIN number written on a piece of paper. When she went to her room that day, she found it right where she had left it.

"See, the card is here!"

What was going on? I started to wonder who could have done it.

A week or two later, Jose came home very late—it must have been well into the early hours of the morning, and he was completely fucked up. His face was red and swollen, like he had been in a fight and gotten punched. But what struck me most about Jose's appearance that night was that his hair was long with extensions.

I knew that he took my makeup and clothes. I knew that he kept a stash of wigs and other items in the basement. I knew that he was discovering himself through friends like Miranda, and though he hadn't directly come out and said to me "I am transgender," he was letting me in on his discoveries, and I could tell that something was there, though I didn't know exactly what. But seeing Jose that night, dressed in women's clothes and with extensions in his hair, was a first for me. I was taken aback. And I was deeply disturbed by the pain and torment written all over his face. More than anything, though, I was fed up.

"Jose, what is going on? You can't be partying like this—you aren't even eighteen years old!"

He was bent over the toilet, heaving. I pulled his hair back and held it away from his face while he emptied his stomach. When he was finally finished, he broke down. "I'm a bad person," he cried. "I'm such a bad person!"

I thought about how guilt can eat away at a person's sense of self. How, with a guilty person, you don't need to say anything; you just have to wait for the guilt to cause them to spiral out of themselves. I was reminded of *Crime and Punishment,* one of my favorite novels, and its protagonist Raskolnikov. After committing a double murder, Raskolnikov's guilt eats away at him until he unravels. That night, I was watching Jose's unraveling, and I had the distinct feeling that he needed me to say the words for him. For me to say, out loud, what he couldn't admit: that he took the money, that he felt awful about it. It was almost as if he was wanting to get caught.

But I was ashamed to have these kinds of thoughts about my baby brother, and so I tried to push them away. I didn't know who Jose was hanging out with, or what he was getting himself into, but none of it felt right. And because of this, I did question whether he had been the one to take the money. The reality was that he had been out with his friends a lot. *How was he paying for it?* I wondered.

Deep down, I knew what was going on. But I was in no state to confront it. I couldn't say those words out loud, put them out there into the universe, because it would have somehow made it easier for him. It would have somehow released him from his responsibility to confess. At the same time, I didn't want this to be the truth, so I convinced myself that he would never do that to our parents. I felt so dizzy just taking in what I knew to be crystal clear.

My parents' neighbor had their ground floor apartment available for rent. I was hesitant about it right from the start; my husband and I could barely afford to give my parents the small amount of rent we were paying them, and anything more seemed risky and irresponsible. But my husband was insistent, convinced the neighbor to give us a deal, and we moved into the apartment next door to my parents' house, just across the *yardita*. The layout was exactly the same—four bedrooms, two bathrooms—but the contrast between the two homes could not have been greater.

My parents' home was bright, full of natural sunlight. It was well kept, newly painted. Cheery. With fresh yellow roses adorning Papi's statue of La Virgen de la Caridad. But just next door, I lived in darkness.

The windows could not be opened. They were old, and never properly repaired, with new screens installed on top of ones that were old and torn. Layers upon layers of stuff you could not see through and that sunlight could not penetrate. The only window that opened just a crack was tiny and new, in one of the bathrooms. The kitchen was old and no matter how much I cleaned, it always felt dingy and worn. I slept in one room, Alina in another, and my husband in a third.

Every time I came home, I felt trapped. The apartment was this constant, physical reminder of how unhappy I was. I was doing theater with this Spanish company, but it wasn't anything that really challenged me or inspired me artistically, and it certainly wasn't supporting me financially. I felt stale. My marriage was absolutely stale. And this house was stale, too.

I hated being there. I would cry myself to sleep, thinking: *This cannot be my life. Just close your eyes, go to sleep. It will be better in the morning.*

But it was never better in the morning. I would wake up gasping, still physically and emotionally overwhelmed by the remnants of whatever conflict went down the night before. I opened my eyes, which, on most mornings, were so puffy from crying that I would need to put ice on them to control the swelling. And when I saw the dark windows, the old apartment, I'd think, *Oh, fuck. This is still my life.*

One particular moment from that time haunts me: I'm driving my Subaru on the highway, and I start to speed. Gradually at first, with a steady pressure on the accelerator. *Just stay here*, I think. *Stay at this pace.*

But my speed quickens. I see a concrete barrier coming up ahead of me.

Keep doing this, a voice inside my head tells me. *Ram into that wall. And it will all be over, just like that.*

I am going to do it. I am going to do it. I am going to do it.

And then, in my rearview mirror, I see my daughter's car seat. Strapped into the rear passenger seat, all innocence and promise. I slow down and, through the tears that consume me, I know I need help. Enough is enough.

I began therapy. If Alina's car seat hadn't been there, I would not be here today.

THE BANK FOUND security footage of a young person withdrawing money from the ATM several blocks from my parents' house. When Mami and Papi saw the video, everything came crashing down.

"Do you know who this is?" the bank official asked them.

"Yes," they said. "Yes, we know him."

"Well, we need to press charges."

My parents panicked.

"No, no, please. Can we withdraw our complaint? Cancel the investigation since we know who's behind it?"

The official sighed. "You don't understand. Stealing that much money is a federal offense. We have no choice but to press charges."

When my parents told me this, it was difficult to take. *How could this have happened?* Everything in my life, it seemed, was falling apart.

"YO NO PUEDO *estar aqui*," my mother cried to Papi and me. "*Esto me va matar!*"

The police were coming to the house to arrest Jose and take him to Central Booking, and Mami decided that she couldn't be around to witness what was going to unfold. I understood this impulse. It was the same impulse I had that kept me from confronting Jose. To be there, or to say something, would have been to acknowledge that this nightmare was, in fact, true.

I was at the house, but I could not physically be in the same space when it was all happening. My father was there, and my brother Tony was there. I remember being in a back room and hearing someone say, "They're here."

And this is where everything goes foggy. This is where my brain goes into survival mode to shut out whatever trauma came next. I don't know where I went, or what happened exactly, but I know I was out of there. Like my mother, I knew that seeing whatever went down between Jose and the police would have destroyed me.

Chapter 13

MARIZOL

. . . .

The cells were in the basement of Central Booking. No beds, just little stools. I remember that it was freezing down there, how I was shivering, how every hour they moved us to a new cell. I was there the whole night with adult men, just keeping to myself, trying not to engage with anybody. I did not talk, I did not eat, I did not sleep, I did not use the bathroom. I had to go so bad, but I held it in because I felt so out of place.

When the police came to the house, I hadn't had a chance to get fully dressed, so I just threw on whatever I could. If I'd had time to get ready, maybe they would have taken me to a women's jail. But other than my hair, long with extensions, and my manicured nails, nothing about me said that I was trans. I didn't yet have my name changed or my gender on my ID changed. But even if I had, it might not have made a difference. Trans folk in jails and prisons are some of the most vulnerable: nearly 40 percent report being sexually assaulted, and nearly 30 percent are placed in solitary confinement for their own protection.[5] In the back of the cop car, I prayed that nothing would happen to me, that the men in the jail wouldn't beat my ass.

I had to remove my shoelaces from my sneakers, and a female officer cut off my nails.

"This is a form of a weapon," she said.

But still, in the cell, the guys could tell I was different, and they made comments about me being feminine, being gay, all of those things I was used to people saying about me at school.

"Oh, here we go! Another faggot!"

Or, "Another wannabe-bitch!"

In that cell, full of grown men, I was scared and uncomfortable, like I was being stripped down. I felt so vulnerable. I wanted to say something to defend myself, but I was afraid that they would have beaten me up. So, I just pretended like I didn't hear them, even though their words were loud and clear.

In the morning, around ten, still having to use the bathroom, I was finally called to appear before a judge. As I walked out of the cell and up the stairs, I saw a trans woman sitting alone in her cell. *Wow, I* thought, *That's me.* I hadn't fully started my transition, but seeing her there was like a sign that I just needed to go for it.

After I received my court date, I left Central Booking, alone and with nothing. I didn't have a jacket or a wallet, and they didn't return my shoelaces. An order of protection had been placed against me, meaning I couldn't go home, but I didn't know where else to go. The sun was shining, and I felt happy and relieved to be out of there. I went down to the subway and showed the MTA agent a slip of paper saying that I had just been released from Central Booking, and he buzzed me through the handicap entrance.

I went to the public restroom in the train station and finally let everything out. It was so painful—my bladder had been stretched and felt like it was going to explode. I couldn't believe what had just happened. I couldn't process anything. All I could think of was that I had nowhere to go. I thought about living on the streets, how ashamed I would feel if people I knew saw me sleeping on a bench in Oval Park. Finally, I swallowed my pride and went to my friend Cameron's. He was someone from the community I met on Myspace when I was just sixteen. He was eighteen at the time, and he happened to live close to my parents' house. I had introduced him to my friends, and he had introduced me to his, and soon we were partying together.

When I got to his house that day, I didn't tell him what had happened with the money. I was afraid of how he would look at me or that his family would think I would do something like that to them, too. I simply told them I had been kicked out of my parents' house for who I was, that I didn't have nowhere else to go. Once I got settled there, Seli offered to pay Cameron's mom a weekly rent and to set me up with groceries so that I wouldn't become a burden on their family. At the time, I didn't know the full extent of all that was going on in my sister's life and how much of a financial burden I was putting on her. I could just sense a distance, a sadness, that she was worried about something.

I **WAS** still living with Cameron and his family when I turned eighteen. On my birthday, Cameron announced, "We're gonna go party!"

We went to the club that night, but it didn't feel like anything special. At that point in my life, we were always going to the club. It was just like any other night. I remember thinking, *Damn, I'm spending my eighteenth birthday like this?* I didn't even have a cake. No one to sing "Happy Birthday" to me. And that's when it hit me how lonely I was: I was turning eighteen, which should have been a huge milestone, and here I was, spending it without my family.

I tried not to think about the situation because it was going to eat me alive. I knew that I couldn't be angry at anyone but myself, and so I tried to make the best of it, but my emotions were all over the place. To say I was devastated by what had happened with my family is a serious understatement. I was also embarrassed and heartbroken. To this day, I don't really understand how I could have betrayed Mami and Papi, the two people who'd always loved me and cared for me, in such a way. Over the years, I had gotten good at ignoring my feelings, pushing them aside and pretending that everything was okay with me, and at school, and at home. But it is exhausting to come off as a happy person—to always be smiling and positive—when you are really hurting inside.

After I'd been taken away in handcuffs, I was forced to confront what I had done, and I fell into a depression. I relied on partying even more as a way to forget all the pain I'd experienced—and all the pain I'd caused my family. But I tried to take advantage of this time I had away from my family. I tried to look at it as an opportunity: no longer living at home, I could finally begin living in public openly as Marizol. I started wearing feminine clothes out in public, and when I got my nails done, I didn't try to hide them. I developed a big personality. I acted like I gave no fucks. I was always jolly, laughing, throwing shade. Being the open, fun, spirited person I'd always wanted to be. And so, though it is difficult to admit, and as painful as the whole experience of taking the money was, I also know that if I had never taken it, and if I had never been forced to live on my own, I wouldn't have had the courage to really begin to live my life as me.

I **DIDN'T** tell Nathaniel about the money either. I felt so horrible for having hurt my parents, and I didn't want him to think less of me. Honestly, even though I was the one who took the money, the whole situation surprised me. I didn't think I was capable of doing such a thing to people I loved, and I didn't want him to think that I was either. I also hadn't planned on telling him about dropping out of school, but that was harder to hide, and he was upset when he found out. He was a successful person—he'd graduated from high school, gone to college, and had a good job. And he wanted the same for me. He didn't want me to fall in with a bad crowd or go down a dark path.

He knew I didn't live at home anymore, though he didn't know why. And as I was discovering myself, I started to show him more and more of Marizol—the hair, the makeup, the clothing. He was still self-conscious about being out, though, and he didn't like the attention I drew to him.

"Why do you have to be so feminine?" he asked me one day. He had picked me up from Cameron's house, and we were driving around the neighborhood like we often did.

"What do you mean? You seem to like it when we're alone."

"Yeah, I do. But do you have to be so out there in public?"

"This is who I am! I'm happy this way."

"Okay," he said. "But why are you always going out in drag?"

That stung. "It's not like that," I said. "I'm not performing. This is just me."

He was quiet. "Yeah, but why?"

I didn't tell him the truth about how I was feeling: that I wasn't just a gay guy going out in drag, but that I was a girl. A trans girl, yes; but a girl nonetheless. And dressing this way, being so out there—well, for the first time in my life, I felt like I was living life as me. I didn't tell him any of this, though, because I think I was afraid of how he'd react or that I'd lose him.

We turned onto Bainbridge, my parents' street. I hadn't really been around since the incident, and I missed them. "Hey, can we just pull over here for a little bit? Like old times?"

He smiled. "Sure."

I was full of so many conflicting feelings in that moment: I was sad that I couldn't see my family, but I was comforted by the sight of their street, the *yardita*, their house; I was afraid to really open up to Nathaniel about why I wanted to dress the way I did and to come out to him as trans, but around him I felt safe and loved. We parked across the street from my parents' house for some time, just listening to music and talking, his arm around my shoulders. I could have stayed there forever.

CAMERON AND I partied nonstop. I got a fake ID from the place I used to take my disposable cameras to get developed. It was not a good fake at all—it said New York State and everything, but it did not look legit. Still, it meant that Cameron and I could go out to the twenty-one-and-over clubs till late in the night. And, most importantly, it used the name Marizol. I started to experiment with drugs like Ecstasy and coke, but it wasn't a habit I let myself fall into. For one, doing coke felt wrong. *This is what my biological mom fell into,* I'd think. Not to mention that the taste made me want to vomit. But I often felt pressured, by Cameron and Jackie, who were always next to me, saying, "Come on! Do it! You only live once!"

Though the partying helped me forget my struggles and pain in the moment, the next day I always felt lonely. Miranda and Cameron didn't get along well, and because I lived with Cameron, I felt like I had to be loyal to him—to leave parties when he wanted, to keep my mouth shut during stupid fights even when I knew he was in the wrong. I tried to open up to him, to talk to him about what it's like to be transgender or how I felt about things with my family. But I always felt that there was a little bit of judgment on his end, a kind of negativity that wouldn't go away no matter how much I tried.

WHEN I was just starting to find myself, to dress and live openly as Marizol, I met a girl at a bar in the neighborhood who was super goth. Emma was always wearing all black—clothes, lipstick, nail polish, the whole nine. Our styles were super different, but the more I got to know her, the more I saw her for the cool, creative person that she was. And she saw me for me, too. She was an artist, musician, and photographer, and around her, I felt safe to explore my creative side. It was something I had always wanted to do but never had the courage or confidence to put myself out there, and after everything that had happened with my family, I was finding it hard to focus on anything other than survival. But when I got together with Emma, we'd talk about ideas we had for creative projects, and it was like an escape from all that I was confronting in my daily life.

She told me that she wanted to do a photo shoot, and she wanted me—Marizol!—to model for her.

"Oh my God," I said. "Really?"

"Yeah, girl! Come on."

A long time before this, I had bought this dress that I'd never gotten the chance to wear. It was like a disco ball, covered in black and silver sequins. I thought of it as my "Freakum Dress," like in the Beyoncé song. I had dreams of wearing it on New Year's Eve with my family. Of course, that couldn't happen, and this dress had just been sitting there, waiting. But now I had a chance to wear it, to get all dolled up like my sisters and cousins would on New Year's Eve.

I added studs and chains to a pair of black ankle booties to wear with a silver tinsel wig. We walked all around the neighborhood finding spots to shoot, and the whole time, I felt a deep affirmation to follow my dreams, to not hold back. Emma was such a special, thoughtful person, and she made me feel special, too. At some point, I put on a second outfit: a purple satin cocktail dress with a purple tinsel wig to match. In Oval Park, I posed by some flowering trees. I leaned against a wrought-iron fence, raised my skirt a little to show some leg. I smoked a cigarette, laid on the hood of a white SUV. The whole time, I felt bold and beautiful. Like I was capable of doing anything.

"Do you have to get so dressed up?" Cameron asked me one night while we were getting ready to go out.

"What do you mean?" I said. "This is just me."

He rolled his eyes. "You're gonna get spooked."

I was the only one in our crew who identified as trans at the time, but no one else took issue with how I dressed or how I presented myself to the world. But with Cameron, there was often a negativity, or an attempt to control how I acted in public. If I was gonna get spooked, he said, he didn't want to be around me. And because I was living with him, I felt like I had to do what he wanted. I felt like his hospitality was something that was held over my head. I was afraid that if I didn't comply with his demands, or, if I didn't show enough appreciation, I'd be out on the streets. Whenever we had an argument and I tried to speak up, he'd make me feel less-than.

"Oh, well, you know that I could kick you out right now, don't you?" he'd remind me. "And then where would you go?"

It was true. I didn't have anywhere else to go. I only ended up staying at Cameron's for two months or so, but it felt like an eternity.

I will always appreciate how Cameron and his family opened their doors to me. Once I asked him and his family to refer to me as Marizol, they never called me by my birth name again. Years later, Cameron came out as trans, too. And I realized that he put me down because he knew that he didn't have the courage to be as open and free as I was at the time. Of course, I didn't know this while we lived together; I only felt the effects of his dismissals.

Often, during those months of living with Cameron, I felt vulnerable, like I had nowhere else to turn. I constantly felt like I was being taken advantage of or emotionally abused. Unfortunately, this is the case for many trans people struggling to find safe, reliable housing. Discriminatory hiring practices make it difficult to find work, and even if you can afford rent on your own, trans folk still fear being kicked out by landlords who discriminate. This, combined with the fact that many trans individuals are rejected by their families, makes any available housing situation feel valuable—even if it means withstanding emotional and physical abuse, or more.

NATHANIEL KNEW where I was staying, and he would pop in on me from time to time. At the hair salon, outside of Cameron's building, outside our friends' building down the block. One day, a group of us were hanging outside of our friend's apartment, just having a good time, laughing and joking and dancing. We had a little bit of cocktails. Some smoke. Some rush that we liked to call Kiki Juice.

I knew Nathaniel's car, of course. But on this day, I didn't pay no mind to the car with tinted windows parked across the street. I was ratchet as hell. There was a big group of us out there voguing, and every time we took a sniff of the Kiki Juice, we'd hold hands and spin around in a circle until we couldn't any longer, and then we were high as kites. Laughing. Telling jokes. Laughing even more because we couldn't control it.

When we finally got ahold of ourselves, Nathaniel rolled down his window. I didn't realize it was him—I just thought it was some random guy from the block tryna holla at us. Feeling bold and free from the Kiki Juice and alcohol and weed, I walked up to the car and said, "Hey, what's good?"

And that's when I looked down and saw that it was him. He didn't say anything but gave me this look that told me he was pissed as hell. My friends knew he didn't approve of this kind of behavior—and once they noticed, they all started yelling, "Oh, shit!"

After Nathaniel left, Cameron said to me: "Oh, just fucking do what you want and leave him! You're mad young—do what you wanna do!"

I really cared for Nathaniel, but in the moment, I thought, "Yeah, fuck that. I'm young! I'm gonna do whatever the fuck I want!" At the same time, though, I knew I was going to lose him.

MY FRIENDS were giving me an outlet to forget the pain I was going through. And, at the time, because they welcomed my transition, I felt like they were supporting me. But we were reckless, and I wasn't always as safe and supported as I thought I was.

The night I woke up in the hospital, the cops had found me wasted, by myself, in Oval Park. Selenis was at my bedside, angry and worried. She told me she was mad about the drugs—but I had no idea what drugs she was talking about.

"The drugs you were taking," she said.

I hadn't been taking any drugs. I'd been drinking, sure. But no drugs.

"Who were you with?"

At first, I was hesitant to tell her the whole truth. "I was with my friends," I said.

"Well, your friends—they left you on the street."

She took me home, to her apartment next door to Mami and Papi's, and I slept it off. The next day—after she gave me coffee and some food—I realized what had happened. Someone in the group I'd been with the night before must have drugged me and left me to be picked up by the cops. I remembered how Mami and Seli used to say to me, "Your friends are not your friends!" How I didn't understand—or, maybe, how I didn't want to understand—what they were saying. This was all too painful to admit to myself, let alone say out loud. But I did tell Seli the truth about what happened.

"I was with Cameron and some other people," I admitted.

She sighed. "Come on," she said. "Let's go get your things."

"What?"

"I am paying that woman for you to stay there, and then something like this happens? No no no."

We made the short drive to Cameron's house for me to get my things. I didn't have that much, but what I did have, I couldn't find, including my envelope of documents. Everything was in there—my passport, Social Security card, ID—but I had no way of knowing who took it and didn't want to make a big deal out of it. I just wanted to get out of there as fast as I could. My relationship with Cameron was never the same after that. We saw each other out every once in a blue and we were friendly, but I always kept my distance.

OVER THE next few years I stayed in several different apartments. First was with a friend of a friend named Paola. She was my age, had a young daughter and a little baby, and had extra space in her apartment off of Grand Concourse. The vibe at Paola's house was so different from the vibe at Cameron's. Her mom and sister would come over a lot, and all of them told me that they were going to accept me for who I was. Living there lifted my spirits, reminded me what it was like to be part of a loving, caring family. They always kept me laughing. And after Nathaniel and I finally had our conversation about our relationship, ultimately deciding to part ways, I was grateful to be around people like them. But after a short time, Paola's mom and sister decided that they were moving in with her, which meant I needed to find somewhere else.

Seli helped me rent a room in the South Bronx, but I could tell that she had a lot going on in her life and that I was only adding to her stress. I decided to move in with Jackie. She and I were constantly partying, going to house parties at an apartment across the street from El Coral. The people there were the types who liked to gamble and do coke. I did neither, but they liked having me around, and sometimes, I'd get the sense that Jackie was jealous of the attention I'd get.

And it wasn't just with her friends—it was with strangers, too. If we were at a club, and guys would eye me and not her, I could tell that she was feeling some type of way about it. She'd make faces of disgust, and I'd try to ignore it, to keep having a good time. More than once, she pulled a guy aside and said to him, "My cousin is really pretty for a tranny, right?"

I started to wonder whether she was really my friend. *Would a friend call me that?*

But still—sometimes it was good with Jackie. We fought like crazy, but she and I were really close, and I am thankful to her for how she opened her doors to me during those years. Late at night, when the clubs had closed and we were drunk as hell, we'd head to Oval Park with Miranda or Lorenzo or a new friend we'd just made. The sprinklers were open, watering the grass in huge, shimmering arcs. We dared each other to run through them, and soon, we were all laughing and cackling and soaking wet.

Chapter 14

SELENIS

. . . .

From the time Jose had been kicked out of my parents' house, I wanted to help him, to be the Big Sister I'd always been. But it was difficult for me. Everything in my life, it seemed, was falling apart. I was falling apart. My marriage was not getting any better. I was a struggling actor doing theater—and theater doesn't pay! There was a time I was collecting unemployment, and I tried to make my unemployment check stretch to support my own family *and* Jose. And I was barely there for myself. Every ounce of energy I had I felt I needed to give to my young child. To get out of bed and take her to school and just be a functional mother. But I worried so much about Jose. Even after I took him to the SVU at the local precinct, I worried that I would get that call in the middle of the night. Even now, years later, I still worry about getting that call. Eventually, I felt like my life was a revolving door around Jose. It was like I was in high school again, and Jose the little boy who held on to my every movement and word.

When it looked like Jose was going to be staying at Cameron's for an extended amount of time, I went over to the apartment to talk things through with his mother. Right away, I was suspicious of the whole situation. *I'm not sure I trust this woman,* I thought.

But I needed to know that Jose had a place to live, and I didn't have time to figure out something else. We agreed that I would bring groceries for Jose, and that I'd pay her a rent of $125 a week.

And then, one night, when I was living in the dark apartment next door to my parents, I got one of those calls I'd always dreaded.

Jose had been found in the park, alone and unconscious. He was in the emergency room at North Central, the city hospital nearby. I was up and out the door.

The emergency room was chaotic and gross. I finally saw him, lying in a bed, wearing a hoodie and baggy jeans, looking disheveled. I remember noticing traces of his other life, including purple acrylic nails, chipped and broken off. It was a life I had known about, but one that he didn't yet seem ready to share with me. I had only gotten a glimpse of it that night he came home to Mami and Papi's, crying and drunk. The staff there was not friendly or kind, and finally I pulled a nurse into the room made of curtains and asked for a doctor. She gave me serious attitude, saying, "You're gonna have to hold on."

Hours later, at dawn, I finally spoke to a doctor.

"Well, he was brought in after being found unconscious on the sidewalk. We found traces of alcohol, cocaine—"

At some point, I stopped listening. I was so angry at Jose for getting himself into this mess. For having me called in the middle of the night because he was doing drugs. *You've got to be kidding me*, I thought.

When we were once again alone, I said to him: "Oh, so you're doing hard-core drugs now?"

"What? No."

"This doctor is just lying to me?"

"But I wasn't."

I could see that this reaction of his wasn't simply him trying to get out of trouble. He seemed sincere. Hurt, even.

"Well, who were you with?" I asked.

"My friends." And then he was the one to become angry.

This could only have meant one thing: "Well, your friends left you on the sidewalk."

That night, I took him home to my apartment and let him sleep it off. He was embarrassed about what had happened, but more than that, he was depressed and angry. Finally, he told me that he had been with a group that included Cameron, and then it was my turn to be angry.

"That's it," I said. "You're never going back there."

FOR THE NEXT several months, my life didn't get much better—and, though we didn't talk about it much, I sensed that Jose's didn't either. But after I got him out of Cameron's, and later into a rented room I paid for, I didn't know what else I could do.

Holidays were especially rough for us all. Because of the order of protection, that first year, Jose wasn't allowed to be in my parents' house. Later, he legally could come, but it was too uncomfortable, so he would spend Thanksgiving and Christmas at my apartment next door. My father was still very angry. "We gave him everything," he would say. And the rest of us were all still dealing with it emotionally. I found it especially difficult to cross the *yardita* with my daughter and husband, knowing that Jose was in that dark apartment, alone, waiting for me to bring over a plate of food.

I used to like holidays, but these were so sad. There were so many years of us all not being together, and being the in-between person took its toll.

That first year, Mami and I didn't make a big production out of it, but we also didn't hide the fact that we were putting together a meal for someone who wasn't there. Papi noticed our movements.

"Who's that for?"

Earlier, Mami had stood up to my father, saying to him: "Fine, Jose doesn't have to come here, but you can't prevent me from seeing him."

And that day, with the whole family there, she looked into Papi's eyes and said, "Jose."

She and I went over to my apartment, and we had our little wine and our little meal, and we just talked. I know that it was sad for all three of us—here we were, in this difficult situation—but we tried to make the best of it. We were there to have a good time, and we did! But there was an underlying sadness that couldn't be completely ignored.

This went on for several years and, over time, I started to see that Papi's anger was more hurt than anything else. As each holiday passed, he started to soften up a bit, and his anger gradually subsided. And then he became the one who would say to my mother, "Aren't you going to take some food over?"

It was then that I started to see a glimmer of hope. Maybe we could all be a family again. With one holiday dinner as opposed to two, with everyone in the same room.

Chapter 15

MARIZOL

. . . .

When I was living with Cameron, I started going to the adolescent clinic at Montefiore Hospital, which was right down the street from my middle school. It was geared toward LGBTQ+ youth, but many people in the cis community went there, too, whether to have a checkup or to get tested for STDs. It was an accepting place, with inclusive posters and flyers pinned around the office. I remember seeing a lot of trans girls in the waiting room and thinking to myself, *Someday, I'll come here for my hormones.*

Dr. Raquel was my primary care doctor for several years before I approached her about hormone therapy. After being forced out of my parents' home, I didn't feel comfortable going to the pediatrician I had seen my entire life. And I didn't want to jump into it. I wanted to do everything the right way. Live in the world as Marizol. Be okay with who I was. I didn't want to physically start changing myself before I understood what it was like to be me.

When I had taken the money from Mami and Papi, part of me thought that I would use it for my gender affirmation surgery. Of course, this was impossible. I had never been on hormones, and I didn't know anyone who had done it before—I didn't even know where to go. Once I was out of the house, I thought about starting hormones, but I was afraid of the side effects—liver damage, increased chance of breast cancer. I knew of girls getting their hormones on the street, but I didn't feel comfortable taking that path. Sometimes, people would trick young trans girls, giving them testosterone pills instead of estrogen. And the medical risks were just too high. I wasn't in much contact with my family, but I always thought about them, about how they'd want me to go about things, take care of myself, be a good, responsible person in the world. I asked myself, *How would my family want me to do this?* Right away, I knew that they'd want me to be safe, to go through a doctor. Finally, not too long before my twenty-first birthday, I felt like I was ready. I couldn't wait any longer.

I'd always felt comfortable around Dr. Raquel, but even though I knew that the clinic was a safe space, I was nervous that day in the examination room. Finally, I got up the courage to say to her: "I'm transgender, and I would like to start taking hormones."

She looked at me and was quiet for a minute. "Is this something you've just decided?"

"What? No!"

"Please understand—I am required to ask these questions."

"I really need this," I said. And then I explained how I had felt this way for as long as I could remember, that I thought it was the right thing for me at this point in my life to begin my hormone therapy journey. I talked for what felt like a long time, and she was there, receptive and listening and kind.

"You know," she said finally, "I've been waiting for this day because I always thought this about you."

I was shocked to hear this. "Really?"

"Yes, really!"

"Why didn't you say nothing?"

"Because I was waiting for you to come to me."

Wow, I thought. *She knew this whole time!* I was so relieved, so affirmed, so seen. I already felt confident about my decision to transition, and this made me forget any hesitation I might have had. I knew this was the right path for me.

"Let's start you off with a low dose of spironolactone, which is a testosterone blocker, and some estrogen as well. We're gonna do low doses because I want to make sure you're on the right track. In a month, we'll do some blood work to check your levels."

I couldn't believe this was happening! I called my sister as soon as I left the office to tell her the news. It was a hot summer day, and it felt so good to have the sun on my face and the wind in my hair. Things were finally going to be different. Finally, I was going to be starting a new life—the kind of life I'd always dreamed of as a kid.

RIGHT AWAY, I wanted to see physical changes. At Jackie's house, I stood in front of the mirror, examining the shapes of my hips, my breasts for any hint of change. Of course, it takes time! That I knew. But I was excited to see the new—the real—me.

For the first month, I took two spironolactone and one estrogen pill every day. I went to Dr. Raquel for my checkup, and again she made me feel like this was the right decision for me. "Wow, you are doing really good!" she said. "Your levels are great, you are looking great! I think this is working for you."

I wasn't seeing the physical changes yet, but I was feeling others. My emotions were all over the place. My first breakdown happened while I was with Jackie, getting ready to go out to the clubs.

"That lipstick looks ugly," she said.

"What? Oh my GOD!" I yelled and starting crying all over the place. Normally, I would have just brushed her off and said, "Girl, bye!" But for some reason her little comment really got to me, and I was a mess.

Ten minutes later, though, I was laughing my ass off.

"What was that?" I asked, wiping the tears from my eyes.

"Girl!" she said. "It's like you're getting your period!"

"What?! No way!"

I wasn't really getting my period. But hormonally, I was experiencing something similar. I was so happy after our little fight. These pills were working. My body was actually changing. Soon, I didn't even mind the crying. *This is a natural thing!* I thought. *Happens to girls all the time!* But it was difficult. I was still fighting my depression, and the hormones made everything feel more intense.

The first physical change I noticed was in my skin. Many trans women's skin becomes softer on hormones. For me, I felt like my skin took on a glow. And then, I saw that my hair was growing, that my face was looking more feminine. I was carrying weight in places that hadn't ever filled out before. I'd hear all the other girls around saying things like, "Yes! I am getting my knots!" I couldn't see anything at first, but when I felt a little firm bud behind my nipple, I knew my breasts were growing.

After about a year of taking pills, I began injections. For the first month, I went to Dr. Raquel for the shots, but I knew that the ultimate goal was to have patients administer the shots themselves, and I felt confident that I could do it on my own. She prescribed me the needles and the syringes, and every other week, I'd give myself an injection on the side of my butt cheek, right under the muscle.

The following day, the site of injection was always sore. And the mood swings were even more intense than they were on the pills alone. Now, I feel like my body knows when it's time for another estrogen injection. I get a little sad. A little tired. I feel emotional about everything. I have mad cravings for random foods. It can be difficult to manage, but for me, it is so worth it.

UNFORTUNATELY, NOT all trans folk have such an easy time getting their hormones. Because a psychological evaluation is typically required before you can begin the process, it can be difficult to find the right therapist who will vouch for your mental well-being. And once you've passed the psychological evaluation, it can be difficult to find a doctor willing to write your prescription. These processes are not only timely but also expensive. Many of my trans brothers and sisters resort to buying hormones on the street, and this is incredibly dangerous— not only because the drugs are unregulated, and you can never fully know what you are taking, but also because of the fact that, for many, sex work is the only way to pay for them. While hormones are just one reason why trans folk may decide to engage in sex work, doing so puts them at risk of becoming victims of violence and even death. This is because sex work, like many other illegal activities, normally happens behind closed doors. What's more, because it's illicit, people engaged in sex work don't report instances of violence or stalking to the police out of fear that they will be considered criminals and prosecuted themselves.

But even with the proper medical care, the simple cost of hormonal treatment can be a barrier for many. When I began my hormones, the gender marked on my identification had not yet been changed, so I was forced to pay out of pocket—around $65 for a month's supply of pills. Injections can cost as much as $400 a month. Luckily, by the time I began my injections, my marked gender had legally been changed, and Medicaid covered my treatment. And this applies to many other kinds of insurance. If more people knew this simple fact, my trans brothers and sisters could live safer, happier lives.

For anyone thinking about beginning hormone therapy, it's so important to seek care from a medical professional. Not only will you be confident in the hormones that you are taking, but also after a physical exam to ensure that you're healthy enough to handle the medication, a doctor will monitor your blood levels and make adjustments to your dosage as necessary. Sometimes, taking too much of a hormone like estrogen can cause your body to produce more testosterone, thus negating the effects of your hormonal transition.

But what I want to stress to my trans brothers and sisters considering hormone therapy is that the emotional effects can be devastating. As trans men and women, we are already subject to so much ridicule and fear—fear of being called out on the streets, of being shamed, of being targets of violence. And once you begin hormones, all of those emotions you feel in response to this kind of aggression are amplified. For many, these emotional side effects are too much, and they stop their hormones altogether. The decision to begin hormones is deeply personal and individualized, but I believe that it is so important to speak to someone—a therapist, a social worker—so that you can have the tools to confront what is emotionally to come.

Today, therapy is an essential tool on my journey of self-discovery and healing. It is hard work, and it didn't magically solve my problems. Some days, it forces me to confront a lot of shit I've worked hard to bury and ignore. But my therapist has given me confidence and taught me that, at the end of the day, I am the only one who can decide what I want out of life. I am the only one who can allow myself to move forward and heal. I didn't have this kind of support when I began my hormones. And though I was aware of the emotional side effects, it was a lonely, confusing, difficult journey. I am grateful for Dr. Raquel for affirming my gender identity and being there to assist me with my hormonal transition, but looking back on it now, I wish I'd had the courage to ignore all of the stigmas and go to a therapist so that I didn't have to deal with those changes on my own.

Chapter 16

MARIZOL & SELENIS

· · · · · · · · · ·

After a major fight between Jackie and me, I needed to get out and find somewhere else to live. I called my brother Tony. He and his wife, Ambar, lived in a one-bedroom apartment and were expecting a baby, but they said that I could stay with them for a few months, as long as I respected them and their rules. Stick to curfew, clean up after myself, no friends in the apartment. I could do that.

Since I'd been living out of my parents' house, I was existing in the world fully as Marizol. This was true even before I began my hormone therapy. But around my family, I toned it down. I still wore makeup and got my eyebrows and nails done—but I wasn't as glammed out as I was when I was out with Cameron or Jackie. My clothes were tight, but more gender neutral. I was still hesitant about them seeing the real me, and I never told them about the name Marizol. One day, Tony pulled me aside.

"Listen," he said. "I don't care that you are the way you are. I really don't care. Just respect the rules, and make something out of yourself. You can be somebody."

I love him so much for this. He is a tough, macho guy, and even though he teased me when I was young, he has always been supportive of me. During that time, though, I still didn't let myself be fully me. Old memories from childhood haunted me: how as a kid, I was always

140

editing myself, worried about how everyone was going to react. Even though Tony told me to my face that he supported me, I struggled with the fact that I still wasn't completely open with my family. I wished that I could have been myself, that I could have said to him, "Call me Marizol," but I was too afraid. My family meant so much to me, I think I was especially afraid of being rejected by them. And the fact that I was back living with them and being called by the name given to me at birth made me feel like I hadn't really gone anywhere over the past few years, like I hadn't really grown. My depression worsened.

When it was almost time for the baby to be born, and I needed to find somewhere else to live, I decided to go back to Jackie's. We had our issues, but I decided we could make it work. And with her, I felt comfortable living fully as me. I saw my twenty-first birthday as a chance to make a fresh start. It was a new year, and I could be a new, happier me. I planned to celebrate at Lucky Chengs, the famous Drag Queen Cabaret in Manhattan. I wanted my sister and our sister-in-law Melodie (Melo, for short) to come out with me and my closest friends. I wanted them to finally meet Marizol.

But I was anxious. I worried about what they would think and whether they would still accept me.

. . . .

I WAS NERVOUS when Jose invited me to his twenty-first birthday party. I knew that I'd be meeting Marizol for the first time, and I just wasn't sure if I was ready. Jose would say to me, all excited, "Girl, I cannot wait for you to meet Marizol!"

And I'd reply enthusiastically: "Yes, I can't wait either!"

But deep down, I was hesitant. *Oh my God*, I thought. *I'm losing my baby brother.* And on top of everything else going on in my life, I worked myself up about it.

How am I gonna be okay with this?

I was afraid that I would say the wrong thing or that I would stare too long or that I'd use the wrong name. But looking back, I think I was just as nervous to meet Marizol as she was to meet me.

. . . .

THE NIGHT of my party, I wore a gray strapless dress. It was very architecture-like and structured, with a sweetheart neckline, a little collar, and buttons down the front. The skirt was plaid and pleated. I wore gray heels, put bronzer all over my skin, and wore my hair up in a high bun with my bangs swept to the side. I got ready at Jackie's place. She was really into makeup at the time and helped me with my eyeliner. For herself, she decided to go full-out dramatic. Bright blue eyeshadow, thick eyeliner, heavy blush. Emma was coming out with us, too, and she was as gothy as ever, wearing all black.

This was the first time my family was gonna see me all dolled up. The first time they'd see me looking so feminine. It was the first time they'd see me after I started taking my hormones, too. I was so excited. It was my birthday! And I was going out, with my sister, as me.

The three of us walked from Jackie's house to my sister's apartment, which was right next door to my parents'. And this was major. It wasn't yet dark, and here I was, fully decked out as Marizol, on my own block. As we got closer, I started freaking out.

"Oh my God," I said. "Oh my God."

But Jackie kept reassuring me. "It's gonna be okay! She's gonna think you look beautiful!"

"I just need tonight to go perfect—do I look good, girl? I don't look like a man, do I?"

"Oh my God, NO! You look so good. Super classy and beautiful."

My sister and Melo were waiting for us outside with a car.

This is it, I thought.

. . . .

WHEN I FIRST saw Marizol, I was struck by how pretty she looked. I remember thinking, *Wow, she's so happy.* Everything felt natural, nothing was awkward or uncomfortable. We were having a girls' night out—drinking, eating, laughing, having a good time. And I was happy to be there, celebrating Marizol.

At one point in the evening, I looked directly at her, in the eyes. I thought to myself, *I know who this person is.* I saw the same soul that I'd always loved and protected. I felt then that there was no going back to referring to her as my baby brother or as Jose. This was it. *From now on,* I thought, *she is my sister.*

. . . .

WE WERE seated at a round booth beside the stage. The restaurant was very colorful and decorated to make you feel like you were in a tropical place like Thailand or the Philippines. The energy of the crowd was mad enthusiastic, and I was excited to be there with my sister and sister-in-law. I felt like I had my family back. But still, all of these voices were swarming inside my head: *Am I good? What do Seli and Melo see? Do I blend in? Do my shoulders or hands give me away?* It was as if I was back in school wondering if I looked cool enough to sit with the popular kids, worrying if I fit in. But these anxieties were amplified because it was the first time my family was seeing the real me.

The show began, and we were all cheering for the Drag Queens and the Lady Boys as they worked the crowd. Seli bought me a drink, one that was lit up in the middle like fire. I started to feel more comfortable, to let myself get lost in these legendary performances. It was like I was at a Kiki Ball again!

And then on the stage I saw a familiar face: Laverne Cox. She and my sister weren't on *Orange Is the New Black* yet, but I recognized her from years before when I was still in the stages of figuring out who I was. She was a contestant on the reality show *I Want to Work for Diddy,* and she was the first trans person I had ever seen on TV who wasn't being made a spectacle. Seeing her was when I realized that, as a trans person, you didn't have to settle for just being the man in the wig. You could be yourself, and you could be successful. When she came out on the stage, I cheered even louder.

"Oh my God!" I said to my sister. "She's the girl from *I Want to Work for Diddy!*"

And Laverne was going all out, doing splits and kicking high and whipping her hair all around. There is a stigma that if you are trans, you cannot be a Drag Queen. But seeing Laverne perform that night reminded me that trans women also have the right to express themselves, to perform, to be creative. We are all just as valid as anyone else.

After their performances, the girls came around the tables for tips. When the trans performers saw me, they all stopped to say something. "Yaz, girl!" Or, "I see you!" Or "Yes, girl, work!" It made me feel good, like I was connecting with other girls like me. I was happy.

. . . .

DAMN, THIS IS *nice*, I thought.

At the end of the night, when Marizol was walking away with her friends, I said to Melodie. "Wow, she looks so happy."

Melo agreed. "Oh my God, yes!"

I felt that she was finally going to be okay. It was a good night! And look at how happy and beautiful she looked! This was her truth.

For the first time, I thought, *the interior matches the exterior*.

Chapter 17

SELENIS

. . . .

Marizol's twenty-first birthday was, in a way, like the quiet before the storm. Everything seemed calm. As Marizol, she seemed happy. And I was grateful that she had somewhere stable to live.

Meanwhile, for me, I was reaching a boiling point in my personal life. With my career, with my depression, with my marriage. And then, once again, I got a call. This time from Marizol herself. She and Jackie had gotten into another one of their major fights, and she couldn't go back. She was, in a sense, homeless, and all of that happiness and light I had seen at her birthday party had come to a shrieking halt.

You've got to be kidding me, I thought. I couldn't believe that I still had to take care of her—who was taking care of me? But what was I going to do? Let her live on the streets? Absolutely not. And so I let her stay with me, in my dark, suffocating apartment.

After the party at Lucky Chengs, I didn't think I was going to see Jose again. When I met Marizol, I had to come to terms with the fact that I was saying goodbye to my baby brother, and I began to mourn that loss. But then, when she came to my door after the fight she had with Jackie, she wasn't dressed like Marizol. She wore baggy jeans, a big hoodie. Her hair was long but unkempt, hidden under her sweatshirt. I was confused—I thought that Jose was out of my life for good, and then here he was. It felt like I was seeing a ghost.

Now, when I think about this time, I recognize these clothes as Marizol's uniform of depression. When I looked at her, I didn't quite see Jose. Something about her appearance had changed, and instead of looking like my baby brother, she looked like Marizol dressed in Jose's clothes. They weren't the clothes of the Jose I remembered—the Jose I knew was always put together, with a shape-up, eyebrows done, some nice cologne. This was weird to me. This was something new. But I didn't see it for the depression that it was. Instead, I thought to myself, *Well, I guess she's not ready.*

And because we never had the conversation about it, because I never thought to ask her what was going on, I reverted back to calling her by her birth name and referring to her as the gender she'd been assigned at birth. Now, I know that this is incredibly hurtful to someone who has mustered up the courage to be his or her true self around the people they love. She had shown me Marizol, and I wish I had had the tools and the resources to recognize that Marizol was never going away, no matter what clothes she was wearing. But I didn't. And I can't imagine how painful it must have been for her to have me call her by that old name.

"Jose—I need you to be home by eleven."

"Jose—I need you to not sleep in all day."

"Jose—I need you to clean up after yourself, to not leave dirty dishes all over the house."

And precisely because it was so painful, from this moment forward in the text, I will be referring to Marizol as Marizol and using feminine pronouns (*she/her/hers*), regardless of how she was dressed or how I thought of her at the time.

DURING THOSE ROUGH months, I wanted some sense of progress from Marizol, to see that she was bettering herself. But she wasn't following my rules. My family told me I wasn't helping her, that I was too weak, always giving in. But what else was I supposed to do?

And then, one night, she showed up well past curfew, maybe around one or two in the morning. She rang the bell to get in, waking me up, and by the time I got to the door I had decided I had had enough. I had tried everything, but nothing was working. I remembered what my family had said about giving in too easily, and I thought, *You know what? They're right. I am a sucker.*

It was time for tough love.

"I told you I wasn't going to put up with this," I said.

"But, I—"

"No way. You can sleep in the park."

The next morning, I learned that my husband, who worked overnights and came home around five or six in the morning, had found Marizol on the steps of the porch and let her in.

She slept well into the afternoon, and when she finally got up, I told her: "This is not gonna work."

An acquaintance of mine had given me some information about a transitional shelter in downtown Manhattan for LGBTQ+ youth. I decided this was our best option. I knew it was going to be hard for Marizol. At my house, she had her own room with a TV. She had her privacy. But she was going to have to deal with it. We couldn't keep going on like we were. Didn't she see how hard the situation was for me? I psyched myself up. I said to myself, *Don't be such a wuss, Selenis. She needs this. It's time for tough love.* The current situation was hurting her more than it was helping. And it was killing me.

I told Marizol to get her things. She was going, and that was that.

WE PULLED UP to what looked like the outside of a homeless shelter. A line of young people wrapped around the building. I didn't want to think about what might have been in there. I was so angry at her. And I was also angry at myself for being so weak, for letting it come to this.

She got out of the car, and I said, "Don't you dare come back. I don't care what it's like in there. You're gonna have to suck it up and deal with it."

On the drive home, I didn't let myself think about what she was walking into. I didn't want to overthink this or second-guess myself. *This is it,* I thought. *You made a decision. She needs to deal with it.*

When I got home, I was overcome with a sense of relief. Finally, I had my space back. I could be there for my daughter. I could start to work through things with my husband. I started to make dinner, and that's when the doorbell rang.

I opened the door, and it was Marizol.

"You don't understand," she said.

She explained how there was no privacy—just a big open space and rows of cots. How it was dirty. How a mouse was walking around out in the open, not afraid at all of the people or the noise. It sounded like a nightmare.

"Well, we're gonna have to figure this out because you cannot stay here."

Looking back, I am ashamed I reacted that way. But I had come to a breaking point. I was done.

"Okay," she said. "I'm sorry."

But nothing changed. She came in and went right back to watching TV in the guest bedroom, sleeping in until well past noon.

A few days later, I vented to a friend of mine. He told me about the Ali Forney Center, how it was more than a shelter, it was an organization that helped young people like Marizol get on their feet. I took down the information and called as soon as I could.

Chapter 18

SELENIS & MARIZOL

. . . .

Maybe it was raining.

As time passes and I think about driving Marizol to the shelter in Brooklyn, I can't really remember with certainty the weather, or the station that played on the radio in my red Subaru. But the feeling—that I know.

I found it hard to breathe that day.

Marizol grabbed her bag and took it to the trunk. She was wearing a big, baggy hoodie, the kind she always wore around the house. We got in the car and drove to Brooklyn, just me, Marizol, and my Pucca doll hanging from the rearview mirror. We didn't really say anything to each other; no small talk, no chitchat. The few times I did speak, I tried to convince Marizol that this was going to be good for her.

"You're going to get your GED."

"You're going to get a job."

"They're going to help you get your own place."

"You're going to be surrounded by people who are like you, who will understand you."

"This is going to be good."

Of course, I wasn't really trying to convince Marizol. I was trying to convince myself.

. . . .

My sister and I didn't talk much during the drive. A few words here and there. Around that time, things had become tense between us. I was feeling depressed, not taking care of myself like I wanted to. And on top of all that, after all that I had done to show my sister the real me, she had gone back to calling me by my birth name. Again, I was toning things down, not just for her but for the rest of my family too. And I couldn't express to her how painful it was to be called that name, how small that made me feel.

I remember that it was raining and we were listening to Spanish music loud. I felt like I was walking onto a stage, in front of an audience of ten thousand people. The butterflies fluttered and fluttered. The shelter was in Brooklyn, far from where we lived in the Bronx. We came to an area with big, industrial buildings, and I was surprised when I heard the GPS announce: "You have arrived at your destination."

We got my stuff out of the car, and my sister said, "Maybe this will be nicer than we expect."

The last shelter she took me to was supposed to be for LGBTQ+ people in between homes. But it was a disaster. No order, no privacy; just cots on the floor of a church lunchroom. Along the walls, there were these metal shelves for storage, and sitting there, among the bags and hats and what have you, was a mouse, just chilling. I saw myself sleeping on the floor, surrounded by dozens of other people, a mouse skittering over me. No way could I live like that. My sister had told me that I had to stay, no matter how bad it was. She told me I could not go back with her. But I couldn't stay in a place like that.

And then I felt guilty. The other people at this shelter probably didn't have any other home or family to go back to. LGBTQ+ youth in general, and trans youth in particular, are especially at risk of becoming homeless. Who was I to go in there, get disgusted by the conditions, and immediately leave? I didn't want to make them feel bad, to think that I was bougie, that I thought I was better than them. To be honest, I felt I was heading in a similar direction.

When I arrived and walked inside that first shelter, check-in wasn't for another two hours. I stood there, conversing a bit with a few people in line. After a while, I said, "I'll be right back. I'm gonna take a walk."

But I didn't go back. I took the subway uptown, to my sister's home in the Bronx, right next door to our childhood home. I was a mess. *How had I gotten to this point? What was I doing with my life?*

When my sister found me on her doorstep, she was so mad.

"You've got to be kidding me," she said.

I begged her: "We'll look for another option." I said, "There is no way I can stay there. You would never stay in a place like that. Please."

A few weeks later, a good friend of hers recommended I meet with some people at the Ali Forney Center, an organization that protects LGBTQ+ youth from the dangers of homelessness and empowers them to live productive, independent lives. Before I walked into the center's main office in Chelsea, I watched as a lot of different people came and went. They were all smiling, looking happy. I thought, *Okay, maybe they are doing something good here. Maybe this will be different.*

I learned that the center isn't only a shelter but also a foundation. A place for LGBTQ+ youth to get help and find support. There, you can get medical assistance and help finding a job. They'll help change your name, get new identification. It seemed like a place where I could feel safe. And so when I got the call from the center telling me they had found a bed for me, I decided that it was the start. The start of me being 100 percent true to myself.

When I stood outside of the building that night beside my sister, my suitcase in hand, I thought to myself: *This is it. My last chance to get my life together. My last chance to fight for my truth. To be a warrior.*

I had to make it work.

. . . .

DURING THAT DRIVE to Brooklyn, I was real with Marizol. I remember saying, "You have to listen. This is it—you have to give this a real try. You cannot walk away from this opportunity. You can't. Because I'm done, I can't do this anymore."

I don't even remember if she responded to me. The air in my car was tense, awkward. My Pucca doll dangled in front of me, with her rosy cheeks and sweet smile. I glanced at her and thought, *Girl, I don't know what's going on here either.*

· · · ·

INSIDE THE building, the hallways were painted white. It was so bright—I felt like I was walking into a tunnel of light.

We rang the bell. Ms. Kane, one of the caseworkers, answered. "Hi, are you Jose? We've been expecting you."

I knew what going to the shelter meant for me, but in that moment, hearing my birth name stung. If my sister hadn't been around, I think I would have corrected her, but it was getting late—it was nearly bedtime—and my new roommates were standing by, waiting, eager to greet me.

Ms. Kane led us into a very large space with high ceilings and wood floors. It was homey. My roommates showed me around: the large living area, the large kitchen, the bathroom, the spiral staircase that led down to the beds. They even offered to carry my things down to my room. Everything was so clean and put together. I felt like I was in college, moving into a big dorm I would share with other young, excited people. This seemed like a place where I could grow.

· · · ·

WE HAD TO hurry to get inside of the huge building. It was nighttime, and we had to be there before curfew. We got in the elevator, and again, it was all silence. The door opened up to this kind of loft space, and I could see a kitchen right away. It was big and clean—very clean. The space was inviting, and I thought, *This is somebody's home.* I felt okay leaving her in a place like this. But as I went down the elevator and out the door, it was getting harder and harder to breathe. I wanted to scream. No, I needed to scream. *She doesn't belong here! She has a family!*

I thought about turning back and getting her, bringing her home. Instead, I sat in the car for a long time, just me and Pucca. Finally, I heard it. Like thunder. The dam broke. I was crying, hard. The passenger seat was empty. And drops of rain pounded against my windshield.

I called my brother Tony. I told him what I had done: how I had left Marizol at this place, how I felt guilty, horrible.

"I'm a bad person," I said. "I'm a bad sister."

Tony is not big on words. But then he said to me what I had been saying to Marizol: "It's gonna be good. This is what she needs. It's time for her to be on her own and it's gonna be good, you'll see."

And I remember saying over and over, "I think I'm a bad person. I think I failed her."

"No," Tony insisted. "It's gonna be good."

· · · ·

Lights out was at ten o'clock sharp, and I was relieved to finally have a structure to my day. When I lay my head on my pillow that night, I remembered a conversation Mami and I had after everyone found out that it was me who took the money.

She told me that she forgave me, that she wasn't angry about what I had done. I remember us talking about what was to come with the police and the courts, and she said to me, "It will be okay. But always pray. Just always pray."

And that night, in my new bed at Ali Forney, I prayed.

I prayed about what I wanted to get out of this experience, what I had come to the center for. I prayed about everything that had happened in my life, about what I could do to change everything I'd done. How I could become a better person, a better version of myself. I wanted to do right, to make changes in my life and have my family forgive me and accept me for who I was. I asked God to forgive me and to keep me strong. Mami's voice was like a refrain in my head: *Do good. Be strong. Always pray.* And I promised to do just that.

As I prayed, I started to tear up. But it wasn't out of sadness or fear. It was out of relief. I was finally in a place in my life where I had hope. There would be no more hiding Marizol from my family. No more editing my truth. This, I decided, was the beginning.

Part III

MARIZOL

· · · · · · · · · · · · · · · · · ·

Chapter 19

MARIZOL

. . . .

When I woke up the next morning at the Ali Forney Center, I had a smile on my face. I felt calm and reassured, hopeful even. Something told me that I was going to be good and that this was a space where I'd find people who wouldn't judge me. I was on a new journey and being guided by a brand new light. Finally, I was at peace—with myself, with all that I had done, with all that had gone down with my family, with everything in my life. I had the chance to get my life together, and I was going to better myself.

I wanted to take over the world, and I didn't want to waste any time. *What's my task for the day?* I thought. I was ready to do what needed to be done: to get my name changed, to apply for government assistance, to look for a job.

Normally, it took me a few days after meeting someone new to feel comfortable enough to open up and show them the real me. But that morning, after I got out of bed and showered, I put on my feminine clothes. As I stood by the mirror to do my makeup and hair, Ms. Kane approached me. I waited nervously, hoping that she wasn't going to call me by my birth name like she had the night before.

I always dreaded moments like these. Whenever I went to appointments or when I was running errands at government offices, I would write down "Marizol" when I could. But if anyone ever looked at my ID or at my official papers, they would always call out my birth name. Those moments were not only degrading and embarrassing but also drew attention to me and made me feel unsafe. When my birth name was called, suddenly I wasn't just the woman in the waiting room—I was the woman with a man's name. I felt like all eyes were on me, like everyone was thinking that I was a weirdo or a freak. I knew I had to eat it up, to keep my cool; if I went off, I would draw even more attention to myself.

A few months before living at Ali Forney, I went to a Social Security office in the Bronx to have my gender marker changed from male to female. Doing so offered me an added sense of security and affirmation. And it gave me a much-needed sense of privacy. If I hadn't changed my gender marker, any time I had to show ID—at the bank, at a bar, to a police officer—the fact that I am transgender would be made public, for all to see.

In addition to ensuring my security and privacy, I needed my gender marker changed because I was finding it difficult to pay out of pocket for hormone therapy. My health insurance would cover it only if my gender marker was female. Dr. Raquel explained to me how to go about making the change, and I brought along with me all of the required documentation, including a formal letter from her explaining that I was transgender, that she had been treating me for so many years, and that the gender marker in my records should reflect my gender identity, not the gender I was assigned at birth.

It had taken a lot for me to muster up the courage and go to the Social Security office that day—as a trans person, even though I know my rights, I always anticipate the worst in situations like those. I fear that I will have to interact with an individual who thinks that being transgender is a choice or who doesn't "believe" that it is a biological, scientific fact. I fear that I will be confronted by someone who makes comments that make me feel uncomfortable or unsafe. I fear that I will have to defend myself against someone who wants to physically harm me because of who I am. Unfortunately, that day, after saying my birth name out loud, the Social Security agent took one look at my papers and said, "I'm sorry, this isn't allowed—I cannot help you."

"What do you mean?" I asked. "All of the documents are here."

"There's nothing I can do for you."

"But, I have—"

"I'm sorry. I can't."

I was shocked. I had everything necessary to complete this process. I couldn't believe that she was treating me this way.

"Can I speak to your supervisor?"

She sighed and called the supervisor over, and I got the sense she was relieved that she didn't have to be the one to deal with me.

The supervisor came, and I explained the situation. I showed him all of my documents, and I told him that this was my legal right. I felt so proud for standing up for myself. It was like I was my own lawyer. When I finished speaking, he looked at his employee and said, "So, what's the problem here?"

She just sat there and said nothing. Finally, she made the change and gave me the paperwork I needed.

Thankfully, that first morning at Ali Forney was different. "Hey, good morning," Ms. Kane said to me with a smile. "I want to ask: how do you identify, and what are your pronouns?"

Yes! I thought. This was the first time in my life someone had asked me these questions, and I was thrilled.

"I identify as transgender, and my name is Marizol. You can use female pronouns: she/her/hers."

"Okay, great. It's nice to meet you, Marizol."

The kids around me were listening, and after Ms. Kane left, they came up to me.

"That's a pretty name!" said one boy named Louis. He and I would become very close. He was gay and super feminine, and we always joked that he was my daughter, and I, his mother.

"Oh thank you!" I said. "It means Ocean-Sun."

"Wow," he said. "You definitely look like a Marizol!"

Chloe, another trans girl, approached me. "Now I don't feel alone! I have one of the girls here with me!"

"Yes, girl!"

I couldn't believe how easy it was or how natural this all felt. Here I was, with people who could not only relate to me but also accept me for me, without any judgment. Up until this point, I had never been in a living situation with people who were so open and inviting. I had discovered who I was through other trans girls I met like Miranda, but because trans people often have to live on the edges of society, away from their families or support systems, a kind of survival mode can dominate many friendships. On the streets, I saw trans women betray one another or criticize each other about their looks or ability to pass as cis-women. Because I was young and on my own, I was often afraid of being stepped on by the more experienced girls. I tried to learn from them and be accepted by them, but still, I kept my distance.

But from the first moment I walked into Ali Forney, I felt warmth and support and love. Everyone was so welcoming and inviting. It felt like home.

Soon after, I went to go meet with my caseworker. I was waiting in the computer room, where residents could work on their résumés or job applications, when I heard someone say, "Marizol?"

It was Natasha, my caseworker. Ms. Kane must have spoken to her, telling her not to use my birth name.

Oh, shit! I thought. *Y'all on point!* I felt even more reassured that I was in the right place. That good things were going to come from my experience at the center.

NATASHA WAS an amazing influence in my life. She is the reason I was able to get my life together. She was always spot-on with anything I needed help with. After I explained my situation, our relationship opened up, and she became not only my caseworker but also my mentor. When I spoke to her about my problems, she gave me advice, always grounding me. Her presence was nothing but positive.

She'd tell me things like, "You are here for a reason."

Or, "You are gonna get your life together."

Or, "Just keep doing what you need to do. I'll be here, keeping you on track."

I met with her every week, and every meeting, she helped me further my goals. She helped me fix my résumé and apply for jobs. She put me in touch with Americe, an attorney from the Urban Justice Center, a nonprofit organization that offers free legal services and advocacy for those in need in New York City. Americe would represent me at the hearing to have my name legally changed, and the Urban Justice Center would cover my court fees.

In addition to meeting with Natasha once a week, the Ali Forney Center provided me with a foundation of support to begin living a stable, independent life. The center sets up a savings program for its residents—with every check you received from a job or government program, the center withheld a small amount and deposited it into a savings account for you. Then, when you were ready to move out, you had enough put away to pay for the deposit on your own apartment.

We were also required to attend group therapy sessions, where we discussed our experiences with issues like discrimination and self-doubt. Before joining the center, I had never heard people speak so openly about their emotions. Hearing other people's stories made me feel less alone and also more sympathetic to others. It was reassuring to know that we were all going through the same things.

But more than anything, I think being part of a community like this gave me a kind of confidence I'd never had before. We didn't really have any cattiness or bad feelings among us—it was always love and support. Being apart from my family for so many years was lonely and difficult, especially around the holidays. But at Ali Forney, we became like our own little family. And even when it was hard, or when I was feeling especially down and missing my parents and siblings, I knew I had others around me who cared, and for that I will be forever grateful.

I SPENT about a year at the shelter, and for much of that time, I wasn't really in contact with my family and friends in the Bronx. I spoke to my mom and sister on the phone occasionally, but I knew that I needed to go through this process of growth on my own. And I didn't want anyone to see me until I was ready. On my birthday, I decided to make the trip up to the Bronx to see my sister and Jackie.

Going on the train always causes anxiety for me. In general, entering any kind of public space causes anxiety. And I'm not alone in this feeling—many of my trans brothers and sisters experience this, too. Because we are constantly mistreated, discriminated against, or harassed, we find comfort in the private spaces of our homes, where we can fully be ourselves. At home, we don't need to worry about what anyone is going to think or say or do. It's draining to constantly live like this. To worry, every time you leave your house, *What's gonna happen to me today?*

When I was living in Brooklyn and going back up to visit my old neighborhood in the Bronx, that anxiety was always present, and the closer I got to the area where I grew up, my fears became worse and worse. *What if someone recognizes me? Will they call me out by my birth name? Am I gonna get spooked?*

A few days before my birthday, Jackie had sent me a message:

It's your birthday! Come by, I wanna see you!

When I got to her apartment, she and her parents greeted me with a present and cake.

Even though Jackie and I had our ups and downs, I loved her like she was my own sister—God knows that we fought like it, too! Her parents had always been welcoming and accepting of me, and when I lived with them, I called them "Mom" and "Dad." Still, I never expected them to do something like this for me. I thought that this birthday would be like all of the other birthdays I'd celebrated without my family—nothing special, just another day. I was so touched, I started to cry.

After a few hours with them, I went over to my sister's house. Selenis had a gift and a cake for me, too. But I couldn't stay long. The center had strict rules, including a seven o'clock curfew, and I needed to be back. I hugged my sister, thanked her, and prepared myself for the long train ride back to Brooklyn.

I got back to the center just in time, and when I walked in the door, everyone yelled "Surprise!"

Arroz con gandules, Puerto Rican–style barbecue chicken, and a birthday cake were all set out, and big Mylar balloons that said "HAPPY BIRTHDAY!" hovered nearby. They even had a few gifts for me. Louis had put it all together, cooking all the food and getting all the other residents onboard. He and I were close, but still, I couldn't believe that he would do something like this for me. I had spent so many birthdays alone, or with people who didn't care much about me, and this year, I had three different cakes. I teared up again. I was so happy to be there, and I was so appreciative of being a part of this caring community. I didn't feel alone. I felt safe. I felt understood.

ON THE way to court to get my name legally changed, I had butterflies in my stomach. I was nervous, but I was happy at the same time. Once I received the court order, I could have both my gender and my name on my documents be true to me. Then, I wouldn't be embarrassed or afraid whenever I had to show someone my identification. *Yes, finally!* I thought.

I met my attorney, Americe, who was there with a few other trans girls who were getting their names changed as well.

She asked, "Are you ready? Are you excited?"

"Yes, girl! I am so excited!"

Once she filed the paperwork, we sat in the courtroom until the judge called us forward.

The judge was an older white man with gray in his hair, and I'll admit that I was intimidated by him. I was afraid of what he would think of someone like me. But when he called us forward, he was nothing but kind. And he called me by the right name! He told me "congratulations," and I said, "thank you," and then it was over, just like that.

When I walked out of the courtroom, I felt like a new person. I was so happy, you'd have thought I was walking down the aisle on my wedding day! I was laughing and smiling.

"Oh my God, Americe, thank you so much!" I threw my arms around her and gave her a big hug.

"Of course, Marizol. This is a big day for you!"

Yes, it was! But it wasn't the end of the process. I still had to go back to the Social Security office and to the DMV and to the insurance company. And I still worried about the kind of mistreatment I might face.

Unfortunately, this second trip to the Social Security office was no different from the first. Another judgmental look. Another "I'm sorry, I can't help you." This time, though, I didn't have the energy to defend myself. I was too drained. So I called Natasha, and she demanded to be put on the phone with the supervisor.

After I handed the supervisor the phone, I could tell by her face that Natasha was going off and letting her have it. It is against federal policies to treat transgender individuals this way. Social Security employees, for example, must treat you with respect and fairness. They must use your preferred gender pronouns and not ask inappropriate questions.[1] And even though government offices provide training for federal employees, many employees refuse to follow the mandatory protocol.

When she hung up the phone, the supervisor apologized. She gave me my paperwork, and then I was out.

But that wasn't the last step. I still had to change my name on my ID and with my insurance company. And each errand stirred up anxieties that still get to me this day. *Is someone going to say something? Is someone going to spook me? Will someone deny me service because of who I am?*

What frustrates me is that I am not asking the entire world to accept me. I know that there will always be people who think that my identity is something unnatural or that I just woke up one morning and decided to live this kind of life. But this is not a choice. It is something that my trans brothers and sisters and I have to live with every single day of our lives. And we can choose to hide, or we can choose to be ourselves and live our truth.

It is not easy being trans—I've often thought about how much easier things would have been for me if my physical body had always matched my mind and soul. When I was growing up, I wished that I could just wake up as a girl. Now, I wouldn't change who I am for anything in the world. Being trans has taught me things most cisgendered people never have to face. I value my perspective and insights, and I am proud of being part of such a resilient and creative community.

So, though acceptance would be nice, what I am asking of the world is that they respect me and everyone else who is part of my trans family. Treat us like any other human being who comes through the door. Our lives are just as valuable, and our rights are just as valid.

Chapter 20

SELENIS

. . . .

The day after I dropped off Marizol at the Ali Forney Center, I was a mess. I cried that entire drive home, and late into the night, and when I finally woke the next morning, my eyes were puffy and red. I felt guilty for having left her there, for not being able to take care of her myself. Most of all, I just wanted her to be okay—I wanted her to be happy and safe and living her life as the person I knew, deep down, she had always been.

Later that afternoon, I got a call. It was Marizol.

"Hi, how are you?" I asked, blurting it all out at once.

"I'm good!" she said. "I slept well, I feel ready to go!"

She didn't just say the words—I could hear in her voice that they were true, and I was so relieved. Here I was, recovering from a horribly stressful and emotional night, and she was sounding good. She was finally sounding happy and safe.

We didn't speak much during her time at the center, but every conversation we had felt like progress. She was hopeful, and though she was probably lonely, being so cut off from the family, she was doing what needed to be done, and I was happy for her.

But I was struggling.

IN DECEMBER 2011, I hit rock bottom. Everything in my life was a challenge: my depression, my marriage, my career. I had tried to make my marriage work for the sake of my daughter, but it wasn't working. At the same time, though, I didn't have any financial stability, and I knew that, as an actor, I wouldn't be able to provide for her on my own. That Christmas, I finally came to terms with the fact that acting wasn't working for me anymore. It was too painful. And if I was going to ever move out of that dark, suffocating apartment and support my daughter on my own, I needed to get a stable job, one with a reliable paycheck and schedule.

Finally acknowledging this was a surreal, out-of-body experience. By myself, on the floor of the living room, the Christmas tree lights glowing softly in the background, I just sobbed for what felt like hours. It was me surrendering to God. I prayed and said, "I know I'm not supposed to be acting any more. I know that I need to stop. This is it."

I called my manager and told her the news. "I don't want to be doing this any longer," I said. "I can't keep doing this."

"You have so much more to give," she said. "Don't worry about it—"

But I couldn't keep going on that way. I just couldn't. "No, I'm done."

Then, in mid-January, she called me with some news. I was getting offers for jobs I had auditioned for in the previous year. "Remember that audition you had for that pilot? Well, you got it!"

I accepted the gig, but it was the first time I wasn't excited about booking a role. Instead, I saw it as a little gift from the universe—a way for me to save money or, at the very least, survive—while I was on the lookout for what I considered to be a "real" job. I went to Los Angeles for about two weeks to shoot, and when I came back, I got two other acting jobs back-to-back. Out of nowhere, it seemed, it all started coming at once. I still had this idea that I was going to give up on acting, but suddenly I was working more than ever.

The following summer, I had an audition for *Orange Is the New Black*. I didn't know what to think about this new "web series" for Netflix—I certainly didn't expect it to be anything magical. But I thought, *Why not do a couple of days on this show? Why not give it a shot?* That first season, I ended up doing eleven episodes, and everything changed.

When I first saw Laverne Cox, I recognized her from *I Want to Work for Diddy* and the performance at Lucky Chengs. And one day, I decided to share with her that I had a trans sister. I was getting ready for filming in the hair chair, with Mamma D, one of the show's stylists. Laverne stood in the doorway and listened when I told her about Marizol. I told her about the support my mother had always showed my sister, and she told me about the support her mother always showed her. It was an immediate connection, and soon, all three of us—Laverne, Mamma D, and I—were crying, sharing this little emotional moment together.

It was only after the first season of *Orange* aired that I realized how powerful Laverne's character, Sophia Burset, was. Jenji Kohan, the showrunner and executive producer, had created a show with rich, emotionally complex characters formed with layers and layers of backstory and experience. And because of the show's depth, and Laverne's performance, I felt that, for the first time, the industry and greater society were actively paying attention to what it meant for someone to be trans. For the first time, I saw a trans character who was married, who had a child, who was treated just as any other human being was and who was as empathetic as any other character.

"Thank you," I said to Laverne months later, "for giving my sister a voice."

She smiled and said, "Well, she's always had a voice."

"No," I said. "She might have always had a voice, but no one was ever listening."

NOW, WHEN I look back on that night I drove home alone from the Ali Forney Center in Brooklyn, I think that without even knowing it, I was saying goodbye to Jose—to my baby brother—forever. That night was the last time I ever saw even a trace of Jose. After Marizol went to the center, I never again had to go back and forth with the pronouns, or with the name. I didn't know she had made the declaration to herself that night that she would never go back to that dark place, living with an identity that wasn't hers but that had been chosen for her, ever again—but I think that I could sense it.

And I began a period of mourning, though I wasn't really aware at the time that that was what it was. I found myself, at random times, crying for the loss of my baby brother. But what helped me heal was seeing how happy and alive Marizol was. I realized that I wasn't mourning the loss of a literal person but the *idea* of a person. And that idea wasn't Marizol's truth—it was simply what I, after all of these years, had gotten used to.

Saying this all out loud now feels strange. Not to mention disrespectful. My family and I accepted Marizol and loved her for who she was, but it was a process for us. And at times, it was incredibly painful. There were so many instances when I would slip up—calling her "Jose" or referring to her as "my brother." It was hard to break the habit. And whenever I slipped around her, she would give me a smile and correct me: "Um, don't you mean Marizol?" she'd say.

"Oh God, I'm so sorry."

What is interesting is that my daughter never slipped. And she never once questioned what it meant to watch someone transition. Adults, I've learned, have a more difficult time accepting change than children do. Adults want to hold on to ideas, to what they've considered to be the truth, no matter how wrong or inaccurate or painful it is to others. Children, however, are much more accepting, much more capable of reframing their views of the world. I never had to have a discussion with Alina about how to address Marizol or how to refer to her; if anything, in those moments when I found it hard to break my own habits, Alina, barely eight years old, would be the one to correct me.

Slowly, I got rid of the pictures of Marizol before her transition that had been out and on display in my home. My mother and I still have them, tucked away in memory boxes, and on occasion, we'll pull them out to reminisce. It is shocking to look at those images today, to see how much Marizol physically transformed during her transition. But what I'm always struck by, and what has always remained the same, are her eyes.

We say that the eyes are the window to the soul, and I cannot agree more when I look at old photographs of Marizol. No matter how much she has changed, or how different her appearance looks now than it did way back when, I see the same person, the same soul, in those pictures, and it's in her eyes. Her eyes are what struck me at her birthday party at Lucky Chengs. Her eyes are what made me think, Oh, *there you are*. Her eyes are what have reminded me that I did not lose anyone during this transitional process. This person, this soul, this human being, this essence has always been there. Even though I struggled with an overwhelming feeling of loss for a time, what helped me most was realizing that the person in front of me was a better version of a human being than what she had been. That Marizol, after her transition, was now a human being who was content, who was happy, who wanted to live.

For family members of trans men and women, I want to say that it is okay to feel a loss in the beginning. But I also want to say that that feeling of loss is an illusion. The person you have always loved and cared for is still there—they are just no longer in hiding. And over time, that feeling of loss will be replaced with the joy that comes with seeing someone you love live their truth.

Chapter 21

MARIZOL

. . . .

The Ali Forney Center was a point of change in my life. It gave me the tools and resources I needed to live an independent, productive, happy life. I was getting things together: my documents had all been changed, I was learning about my rights. I was becoming the me I had always wanted to be. A major goal of the Ali Forney Center is to help its residents find lawful employment. It provides workspaces for résumé revision, and it helps youths prepare for interviews and networking. While I was at the center and looking for work, I applied for a job that appealed to my future career interests and that I had experience for: a prep cook for a company that packaged and sold organic lunches to private schools around the city.

In addition to working at my brother-in-law's family restaurant when I was sixteen, I worked the counter at a sandwich chain in Manhattan one summer in high school. I liked working there—I always had fun with the customers and developed good relationships with the regulars, but I ended up quitting for the same reasons I left high school: I wasn't directly bullied or made fun of, but constant low-key signals made me feel like I wasn't fully welcome.

Thanks to my time at the Ali Forney Center, I now had the tools to cope with the grief and pain that come with constantly being discriminated against and mistreated. What the center couldn't do, however, was change how the outside world treated someone like me.

One of the biggest barriers for trans individuals is finding reliable, steady employment. To put this into perspective, the unemployment rate among transgender individuals is three times greater than the national average.[2] Federal courts have ruled that discrimination against someone who is transgender constitutes illegal sex discrimination, yet there is no federal law banning employment discrimination on the basis of sexual orientation or gender identity, and many states do not have laws explicitly protecting trans folk or the greater LGBTQ+ community from discrimination in the workplace. In thirty states, one can be fired simply for being transgender.[3]

On top of this, discrimination, whether on the basis of sex or race or sexual or gender identity, can be difficult to prove. It requires thorough documentation and legal services, which can be pricey and time-consuming. The National Center for Transgender Equality provides detailed information about trans individuals' rights when it comes to both federal and general employment, reminding us that even if our states have yet to pass legislation banning discrimination on the basis of gender identity, we have the right "not to be fired or refused a job or promotion" because we are transgender. And many legal-aid organizations, such as Lambda Legal, the Transgender Law Center, and the Sylvia Rivera Law Project, can help transgender individuals with legal advice or support.

Personally, I've heard lots of different things when applying for jobs. A lot of no's. A lot of "We've gone with someone else." I've even heard, "We just think that your look would be too distracting to the work environment here."

When I arrived at the organic culinary facility in Harlem for my interview, I was confident and positive. I had the qualifications. I had my new, updated résumé. I had interview clothing. I was ready! And I was determined to get this job!

The interview went so well. I felt comfortable, like I was finally doing something productive to better myself and to live an authentic life. All of my documents had been changed to reflect my correct gender and name, and I felt excited and proud to finally present them to an employer.

"Thank you so much," the woman said to me after our conversation. "We're gonna call you for a follow-up interview."

The following week, I got the call, and I went in for a second interview. I left that day feeling as confident and as excited as I had the week before. It would only be a matter of days before I was working again.

But a few days passed, and then a week, and then a bit longer, and I still hadn't heard back. Finally, I decided to call and follow up. The career counselors at the shelter told us that employers liked that kind of enthusiasm. It showed initiative. It told the employer, "I am serious." And I was serious. If I was ever going to get on my feet, I needed a job.

The woman who had interviewed me answered the phone.

"Hi, my name is Marizol. I'm calling to follow up on a job interview I had last week."

"Yeah, hi," she said. "So, we decided to give the position to someone else—"

My heart sank.

She went on: "We just felt like your presence would distract the other workers."

I was shocked someone would actually say something like that. I couldn't speak. It was almost as if she punched a knot in my throat.

"You understand that we need everyone to be focused here. A lot of our employees are men, we aren't sure if you—well, your look might be a bit of a distraction to the guys here."

In that moment, all I wanted to do was hang up, but I kept my cool. Finally, I came to my senses and said, "Okay, thank you for your time."

It was only after I'd hung up the phone that I thought to myself, *What the fuck just happened?*

I thought about taking legal action, but I didn't have any evidence. I needed to have a recording of the conversation to prove that the reason she didn't hire me was a form of discrimination. Though I understand that evidence is needed in legal proceedings, as trans people, we are always worried that someone is going to harm us because of our gender identity. It is psychologically draining to think this way, especially when we are expected to brush off moments like these and pretend like nothing happened or to get up the next day and try again. And if the only way to protect ourselves is to expect the worst of others and arm ourselves with audio or video recordings before an incident happens, we will reach a breaking point. For me, everything seemed to go so well at the interviews, it never occurred to me that I wouldn't get the job. After getting the news, I was defeated. I was losing hope that I would ever get a job. And I started to fear that I would have to do whatever it took to survive.

I was just eighteen years old when I began sex work.

I wasn't alone. Many people in my community are forced to resort to it. Once I was out in the world, living my life as trans, I started meeting all of the girls. And they understood my situation: that I was without family, without a job.

"Girl, wanna make a coin?"

I had no other way of supporting myself, and so I had a friend of mine put my profile up on an escort services website. It wasn't something I wanted to be doing, but I couldn't let myself overthink it.

There is a misconception that we, as transgender women and men, participate in the sex trade because we are overly sexual people, that we do it for our own pleasure. This could not be farther from the truth. The reality is that we do it for survival. We do it because we cannot find other forms of work. We do it because transitioning—hormones, surgeries, treatments, clothing—costs a lot of money. For most of us, transitioning isn't an option; it is another form of survival. Though we know that we will be subjected to ridicule and discrimination, many transgender folk decide that transitioning is the only way they can feel comfortable in the world. It is the only way we can go on living.

Luckily, the times are changing. Education and greater awareness about what it means to be transgender mean that more young trans people have the support they need to finish school and find work. But still, we have a long way to go. We've seen how those in power continually threaten or aim to demolish the rights of transgender individuals.

There is an urgency now, perhaps more than ever, to advocate for and protect young trans individuals so that they do not fall into the same harmful cycles that I and so many of my trans brothers and sisters have fallen into.

In my experience as an escort, I never received any sexual pleasure. I made money that I needed for food, for rent, for washing my clothes. I made money to help pay for my hormone therapy before it was covered by my insurance. But with it came huge emotional distress and pain. Every time I went out, I felt like I was losing myself. I felt belittled. I felt like I was giving myself up just so that I could pay my bills. I tried to convince myself that it was just like any other job, but it was draining to constantly feel like I would never be accepted in society. That I would never amount to anything other than the "TS"—online lingo for "transsexual"—escort.

I've always dreamed of having a family: getting married, having children. The majority of men who sought my services were men who had families themselves—and knowing this always made me feel cheated. It always made me feel so low because I wanted what they had. I wanted the family. I wanted the kids. I wanted what these men clearly did not value. I wanted the relationship where a man saw me for the woman I am, not just a sex object. But instead of being respected, of being considered a legitimate partner, I was just the chick that was getting paid for someone else's pleasure, for someone else's sexual fantasy. And this fucked with me.

Many people think that we choose to live this kind of life. It's true that deciding to participate in sex work is a choice, but for many of us, we feel as if we have no other option. We do what we gotta do to get by. We do what we gotta do to survive. It is not easy work, and many are afraid to speak openly about their experiences out of fear of being judged. And so we just brush it under the rug, letting those dark memories eat away at us. On top of the emotional risks, the fact of the matter is that sex work is incredibly dangerous. You have to learn to trust your instincts. If your gut tells you that something is off about the situation, you have to listen and get yourself out, even if it means not getting paid.

One night, when I was by myself at a hotel in the Bronx, a man put a gun to my head. I had been working all evening, so he knew I had money stashed, and he wanted to get his hands on it.

He gave me an ultimatum: "I'm going to rape you, or you're gonna give me your money."

The money was enough to cover my expenses for an entire month, but I didn't hesitate. I handed it over.

"Don't even think about calling the cops," he said. "I fucking know your name, I can find you."

He ran out, and though I should have felt safe now away from him and his gun, I was afraid to go outside. I didn't know if he was waiting around a corner for me somewhere. And even if he hadn't threatened me, I wouldn't have called the cops—I would probably have been arrested myself. I was shaking out of fear. I had always tried to protect myself—to always use protection, to go out with a friend, to carry pepper spray. But it just goes to show you that no matter how safe you think you are, or how in control you think you might be, participating in this kind of work makes you vulnerable to violence, extortion, and worse.

Somehow that night, I made it to Jackie's house, where I was living at the time. I was so scared, I couldn't even tell her what had happened. I decided that I wouldn't do any more escorting, that I had to find another way to make ends meet. It was a terrifying situation to be in: earning money as an escort was the only way I knew I could guarantee my survival, but it was putting my life at risk. Still, I knew that I was lucky. Situations like these happen all the time. I knew so many of my trans sisters who had it much worse than me, trans girls who had been assaulted or raped or left in a dingy motel for dead.

I WAS on my way to a job interview, all nicely dressed in professional clothes, when I noticed a guy on the subway checking me out from the other side of the train. He really analyzed me and stared. I became really uncomfortable, but I tried to keep to myself.

And then, I noticed a shift. I can't explain how, but trans folk can always feel it: when someone's gaze goes from "Dayum!" to "Oh, I know what you are." You can always tell when someone knows.

At the next stop, after a handful of people exited the train and even more entered, I noticed another guy staring at me. I tried to ignore everything else and stay calm—I needed to get to my job interview! And I didn't want any trouble. The first guy, the one I knew knew that I was trans, kept watching me. But it was when he noticed the second guy checking me out that he decided to spook me.

"Oh, yo, that's a nigga over there!"

Everyone looked at me. I was so embarrassed. I'll admit that sometimes it can be hard for me to keep my mouth shut. I also know that sometimes saying something smart back can cost you your life. That day, I tried to bite my tongue. But then, something just burst out of me. I looked directly at the man who let everyone on the 4 Train know my business.

"You were checking me out," I said. "Clearly, you like what you saw. I'm over here minding my own damn business, nobody's here for your ugly ass."

That got him angry. He jumped out of his seat and started coming my way.

"Get the fuck outta here," he said. "I'll fucking snuff your face. I don't play that shit!"

I was scared as hell. He was a big guy, and I could tell that he wanted to hit me. So I pulled out my pepper spray and got him right in the eyes. It was the first time I'd ever used it, though it wouldn't be the last. Luckily, right as I sprayed, the train pulled into the next stop and I fled out. I ran down the stairs as fast as I could, just spiraling.

Why did no one say nothing? Why did everyone just sit there watching?

LGBTQ+ individuals are all susceptible to hate violence and crime, but transgender individuals, especially transgender women of color, are especially vulnerable. According to a report by the National Coalition of Anti-Violence Programs (NCAVP), in 2016, aside from the tragedy of the

Pulse Nightclub in Orlando, 68 percent of the victims of hate-violence-related homicides were transgender or gender-nonconforming people. And all but two of these homicides were transgender women of color.[4]

That day, after I ran from the train, I was on the verge of breaking down and crying.

And then I said to myself: *No, no. Not here. Damn.*

It's hard to experience these kinds of threats by yourself. To pull up your Big Girl pants and continue with your day. But that's what I did. I went to my interview, and the next day, I got the call telling me they decided to go with someone else.

TRANS PEOPLE often feel that the sex industry—whether it be escorting, strip clubs, porn, or something else—is the only place that is inviting for us to make money. For me, this kind of work seemed like the only way for me to get a job and be accepted.

Still, it has had its effect on me. It stripped me: of my morals, of what I believed in, of my self-respect. And I felt like nothing. There is a lot I have done that I am not proud of, but I can't beat myself up about it now because it was my reality, it was the only way I knew to survive. But I want my trans brothers and sisters, and anyone else who has had to participate in sex work, to know that, if you want to, you can change your situation. You can get your sense of self back. I know a lot of girls who have completely turned their lives around from sex work and have gone on to do amazing things. They have steady jobs, they are living productive lives, they are happy and at peace. I was inspired by individuals like these.

I knew that I could not be at peace with myself until I stopped. And it was a struggle. Many nights I went hungry. Many times I didn't have money in my pocket to do simple things like laundry or buy groceries, but I knew that, for me, I could just deal with the situation for what it was instead of going back to a lifestyle that put me physically and psychologically at risk. I do not judge or criticize people who decide to live that life, but many are simply resigned to it because they believe there is no way out. And I want to say to them that there is.

ALI FORNEY prepared me to branch off, to be on my own. It gave me the tools and the resources I needed to be independent. For so many years, I had depended on my sister or on my friends, and it felt good to come out of a place that helped me better myself mentally, emotionally, and physically. After leaving the center, I made a promise to God. I promised to be true to myself, to be on a better path. I promised to have a better relationship with my family. And I promised that I would find a job—and give up sex work for good.

I was eligible for low-income housing and found an apartment back in the Bronx. Down the street from where I was living, a restaurant was looking to hire a bartender. I was hesitant at first to apply. I worried that the kind of attention I'd get from men while bartending would trigger the trauma I experienced while doing sex work. But I needed a job. And Natasha's voice was always in my mind, encouraging me to be my best. "Always remember," she'd say, "you have all the tools." And so one day in September, I mustered up the courage and walked into the place and asked to speak to the manager.

I told her about my experience with cooking, about my ambitions of having a career in the industry. It was all going well, but then I felt like I needed to get real with her. "I live by myself," I said. "I have my own apartment, and I have bills and rent to pay. I need to work. Will you please give me this job?"

And she did. She heard me, and she seemed like someone I could learn from. She was a strong, independent woman running her own business. She inspired me, and I felt so blessed.

I never disclosed to the owner, or to the other staff members, that I was trans, and it was liberating when, after I was hired, I could hand over my documents with all of my correct information. For the first time in my life, people saw me for me and treated me like I was just like anyone else. It felt good to work. It felt good being in an environment where I didn't have to worry whether someone was going to call me out by my birth name. I was making money in a safe, legal way, and I felt empowered. I was getting my morals, my innocence, my sense of self back.

Chapter 22

SELENIS & MARIZOL

. . . .

Even after Marizol was out of the center, it took her some time to come around to the family. I knew that she was in a good place with her transition—she was working, and she seemed happy. My husband and I were having a big Christmas party with my in-laws, my parents, my brothers and sisters, and I wanted Marizol to be there, too. A lot of time had passed since the incident with the money, and it always pained me to think how difficult it must have been for her to spend all those years alone, away from us. So many young LGBTQ+ people are forced to spend holidays away from their families, and I didn't want Marizol to keep having to. I remember being so happy that she was finally going to be coming back to us, but I was also nervous as to how everyone was going to react.

. . . .

I WAS so excited when my sister called and invited me to spend Christmas at her house, with my family. I was at such a good point in my life. I was taking control and turning things around—I was working, I had a roof over my head, I was supporting myself, and I was fully into my transition. I was in a much a better place than I could have ever imagined being in before going to the center, and finally, after so many years of being apart from everyone, I felt ready to share my life with them. There would be no more hiding. I felt excited to say, "I am here! This is me!" My job had given me confidence and a sense of empowerment, but it was hard not being able to share that kind of satisfaction and accomplishment with others. I really wanted my family to experience that with me, and now it was finally happening.

But very quickly, a sense of paranoia took over. Seli and Mami were the only people who had seen me since I had moved out of the shelter, and the thought of seeing the rest of my family members made me nervous. *What will they think of me? Will they think I am feminine enough? What am I going to wear?* It was similar to what I felt before celebrating my birthday with Seli and my sister-in-law at Lucky Chengs, but on a much greater scale. I had missed my family, especially Papi. It was really important that he accepted me.

· · · ·

IT IS A tradition of sorts for my mother and I to go Christmas shopping together. That year, when we were going from store to store, with Christmas music constantly playing in the background, she gave me a look and said, "I want to buy something really pretty for Marizol." And I knew exactly what she meant. This would be the first time she was buying presents not for the son she was used to but for her daughter. It was exciting. And we were happy.

We started looking at everything fabulous, everything that was pink: fluffy slippers, soft sweaters, floral perfumes. It was as if she and I were going out of our way to make up for all of those Christmases we had gotten wrong.

· · · ·

ON CHRISTMAS Eve, I went shopping for gifts and an outfit. I wanted everyone to see the real me, to see Marizol, but I also didn't want to overdo it. I remember being in a little boutique, trying on dress after dress, thinking with each one: *Do I look good? Do I look feminine enough? Could I pass?* I didn't want to wear anything too revealing or flashy. I knew that Seli's in-laws were going to be there, too, and though I always felt warmth and acceptance from them, I was nervous about what they would think. Every holiday, the women in my family would dress up in classy, sophisticated outfits, and I wanted to present myself with the same look I had always admired.

Finally, I found a dress that worked. It was simple but festive: a black tank with silver sequins along the front. I paired it with black stockings, a black trench, and Jeffrey Campbell ankle booties I was obsessed with. I wore my hair in a bob and wine-colored lipstick. I felt beautiful and confident, and like me. But still, before ringing the doorbell, I paused and took a deep breath.

Just be yourself, I thought. *Just be yourself.*

. . . .

I DON'T REALLY remember the specifics of that holiday. What I remember is being hyperaware of other people's reactions, of being so tense that I couldn't relax and enjoy myself. I wasn't comfortable in the moment. More than anything, I wanted to make sure that Marizol felt good, that no one said anything inappropriate or offensive or hurtful.

I remembered a story I'd heard as a kid, one that was told, over and over, in my extended family. My uncle, out at a club, had been "tricked" by a trans woman. Every time they told the story, the men gathered around with drinks in their hands, like a males-only club, ready to laugh and holler at the expense of others.

"He got quite the surprise!" one said.

"But you couldn't tell by looking at her!" said another.

Luckily, no one said anything like this to Marizol that holiday. And my in-laws were especially kind and lovely to her. Once they learned about her transition, they were wholly accepting of her, and that night, they used the right pronouns and made a point to be respectful and loving. But I couldn't shake the worries and fears that were brewing in my head, and so I couldn't be comfortable, I couldn't enjoy what became a beautiful, important moment for my sister.

. . . .

WHEN I walked in, it felt like it was just another Christmas. Like no time at all had passed. I felt welcome. No one made me feel self-conscious or called me by the wrong name. I was so happy to be there, dressed up like my sisters and cousins, in an outfit that Seli would have worn, finally free to be me. I felt love in the room in a way I hadn't felt in years. But still, throughout the night, little thoughts drifted in my mind: *Is my makeup okay? Am I pretty enough? Do I have a five o'clock shadow?* And more than about my appearance, I worried whether my family—Papi and Isa and my brother Tito—could really accept me.

Soon, salsa music was playing loud. There was wine and liquor, good food and laughter all over. It was a party! And it was time to dance.

I looked over at Isa, my sibling closest to me in age. When I began my transition, a distance formed between the two of us. I was no longer living at my parents' house, and she wasn't involved in the process of my transition at all. Instead, she was just always watching from a distance. I think that, during those years, Isa felt like she lost me. And that Christmas Eve, I got the sense that she was still processing it all. But once we started dancing, I think she realized—and everyone else in the room realized it, too—that I was still the same person. I was still me. She and I danced, and everyone in the room could feel our emotions building. It was then that Papi walked over to us and pulled me closer to him.

"*Tu eres mi hija,*" he said. "And I love you the way you are no matter what."

I had always wanted to hear this from him. For so many years, I had missed having him in my life. And once I began my transition, it was almost like I was reborn. Like I was moving through childhood and puberty once again, but without Papi there to support me, to give me advice when I needed it.

I started crying. And then Isa started crying. Seli came over and was also crying. And then we were all there, standing in a circle, our arms wrapped around one another, hugging and dancing. It was a beautiful night. It made me feel validated. It made me feel reassured. I had always dreamed about being my authentic self around my family, and finally it was happening. I felt so happy. So blessed and lucky.

Chapter 23

MARIZOL

. . . .

After the warm, welcoming Christmas with my family, things started to fall into place. My job as a bartender was going well. I spent more and more time with my family. My relationship with my parents, my brothers, and my sisters was finally going good. I started to make plans to go back to school, to get my GED. And then, out of nowhere, I met somebody.

I was straightforward with Josh, telling him up front that I was transgender. I also told him that I didn't want to date anyone. I was busy working on myself. I needed to stay focused on the right path. I had just gotten my life back together, and I didn't want to put all of it at risk. On top of that, I didn't want to get my heart broken. I explained this all to Josh, and to my surprise, he was understanding. Supportive, even. And he made me feel comfortable to open up even more.

We decided to go on a date. At first, he said he wanted to come to my place.

"That's not a date!" I told him. "And I don't know you like that. If you want to go out with me, you better take me out."

"All right, cool," he said. "Let's go to the pool hall."

We did. And something about it just felt right. I tried to keep my cool, to make it seem like I was keeping my distance from him, but the truth is that I liked him more than I let on. I knew that I wanted to continue to work on myself, to become the best me I could be—but how many times does love come along? Trans women often feel that no one will love us for who we are. Most guys will just walk away after finding out about our identities, and the ones who don't will usually turn it into a conversation about sex. But here was someone, a smart, understanding, and nice guy who seemed to be genuinely interested in me. And he listened. Also, I thought he was cute as hell. He was kind of hood, with long hair that he'd pull back into a bun or wear in braids.

After the pool hall, he and I went to the iconic Crown Diner, near Yankee Stadium. We sat in the second booth, he with his cheeseburger deluxe and me with my chicken sandwich, and I felt comfortable enough to just lay everything out on the table: about being in foster care, about taking the money from my parents, about living at the center. I never spoke to anybody about these things, and I knew that it was a lot to tell somebody on a first date, but if this was going to go somewhere, I wanted him to have the whole picture of who I was and what I wanted to become. Instead of being scared, he opened up to me, too. He told me about all that he was struggling with, about how he was trying to become a better person.

I had butterflies in my stomach the whole night, but it was a feeling I loved. I had always watched couples on dates, holding hands, or sitting across from each other at a diner like we were that night, and I wondered if I could have that, if I would be able to find someone who accepted me for me. Nothing about that night was extravagant or over-the-top, but sharing that first meal together at an old-fashioned diner in the Bronx was magical. I started to fall for him.

But right away, there were red flags. Red flags that I ignored.

IN FEBRUARY, a friend of mine was celebrating her birthday out at a club. I hadn't gone the year before, when I was still at the center, so I promised her I would be there. When I told Josh about my plans, he was not having it.

"Why you goin' to the club? So you can see other niggas?"

"What the hell are you talking about? It's my friend's birthday! You should come, too."

"I don't have my ID," he said. "It's at my house."

"Well, okay, let's go and get it."

"Nah. At those places you have to dress up fancy."

He was coming up with any excuse he could not to go.

"Oh my God, no you don't. Just put on a nice button-down and some sneakers. It's just the Heights. It's nothing fancy."

He didn't say anything.

"Come on, let's go."

"No. You're not going."

I couldn't believe that he was telling me I couldn't go see my friend on her birthday. But I held my ground. He wasn't going to tell me what to do. I was going to support my friend.

"Fuck you, then," he said. "I'm going home. You're all the same."

We got into separate cabs. I went to the party, and he went to God-knows-where.

Wow, I thought.

We didn't talk for days. Then, on Valentine's Day, he asked me to be his girlfriend. I thought about what had happened, about how he probably believed that his girl shouldn't go out, that she shouldn't have her own friends, that she should always be at home, playing the housewife and submitting. I didn't want to be that kind of girl, but I really did like him. And so I said yes, knowing that was the standard I was supposed to add up to.

VERY QUICKLY, I started losing control over my life. He didn't want me to have social media accounts—he and I had met on social media, so if I wasn't looking for other guys, what I did I need them for? I deleted my Facebook and Instagram. But that wasn't all.

"You need to get rid of that job," he said.

"Why?"

"I can take care of you. I don't want my girl to work."

"Well, I need to work," I said. "I want to work."

"Find another job."

"What do you mean, 'find another job'? It's not so easy for some-one like me. I'm lucky I have this one!"

"I don't want you working there. There are too many guys there. I don't like the way you dress when you go to work. I don't like how they look at you."

"It's just bartending! That's how you make tips!"

But he was insistent, and we started to fight.

Eventually, I gave in. I was his girl. And I had this idea that to be someone's girl, you had to do whatever it was they wanted.

Now, I see how inexperienced I was in terms of relationships and matters of love. Before Josh, my only other relationship had been with Nathaniel. We had started dating when I was just seventeen, before I began to transition. Nathaniel was older than me, but with him, I never felt like I had to do exactly what he wanted. And despite how comfortable I felt around him, how much I felt loved, in the end, he wasn't comfortable with my transitioning, and this broke my heart. I tried to explain to him that I'd be the same person he loved—it was just my appearance that would be changing. Still, he didn't want that, and I held my ground. Instead of doing what he wanted, or letting him make decisions for me, I did what I felt like I needed to do. And then we went our separate ways.

Josh was my first boyfriend since I had transitioned. I didn't know what it meant to be someone's girlfriend or how to stand up to some-one without losing them for good. I also knew that finding someone who could accept and love me for me wasn't going to be easy. I wanted to stick it through and make it work. I knew that he had his own demons, that he had struggled in life, too, and I thought that I could be the woman who could change him for the better. *If it takes me leaving my job*, I thought, *then I'll leave my job*.

I was sad when I gave my notice. Part of me wondered whether I was losing myself again. Now, I see that quitting my job was the be-ginning of me telling him it was okay for him to control me. It was the start of me saying, "Yes, it's okay for you to treat me this way. It's okay for you to make decisions for me." Now, I realize how I was able to then fall into a pattern of abuse that so many vulnerable individuals, especially trans women, fall into.

NCAVP defines intimate partner violence (IPV) as "a pattern of behavior where one intimate partner coerces, dominates, or isolates another intimate partner to maintain power and control over the partner and the relationship." An "intimate partner" can refer to a current or former dating partner or spouse. IPV can take many forms, including emotional, economic, physical, and sexual abuse. According to the Centers for Disease Control and Prevention, IPV affects millions of Americans.

IPV is devastating for all victims. But for those who are already vulnerable to harassment and discrimination, like members of LGBTQ+ communities or those who are HIV-positive, IPV can be especially harmful. And when a victim of IPV also fears homelessness and hate crimes, like so many LGBTQ+ people do, it can feel as if they have nowhere to turn.

Unfortunately, trans women are more vulnerable than other populations to abuse and IPV. Studies show that up to 50 percent of transgender individuals have experienced some form of IPV in their lifetime,[5] and rates are higher for those who have been homeless, participated in sex work, are multiracial, or are undocumented.[6] In NCAVP's 2016 *Report of Intimate Partner Violence,* transgender women were "2.5 times more likely to be stalked, 2.5 times more likely to experience financial violence, and 2 times more likely to experience online harassment" than non-trans LGBTQ+ victims of IPV.[7]

ONCE I left my job, things were okay between me and Josh, at least for a while, and I fell madly in love with him. I opened up to him about everything, including my experience working in the sex industry. He seemed okay with it all, and I was thankful to have someone accept me for me. He told me that he didn't see me as transgender but as a cis-woman. This was all I had ever wanted—to be seen as the woman I always felt I was. Now I think about those comments differently, but at the time, I felt flattered and seen.

It was always up and down with him—one moment, things would be okay; the next, he'd be jealous about some little thing or accusing me of cheating on him. He started to use what I had told him about my life in confidence against me. He threatened to tell my parents about the sex work. He called me a whore. He told me that no one else would love me for who I was or with what I had done.

"You're lucky that you've found somebody as accepting as me," he'd say. "Nobody would ever want you."

Of course he wasn't really accepting. If he had been, he wouldn't have used my past as fuel for his abuse. He wouldn't have belittled me or made me feel less-than. He wouldn't have been ashamed about the fact that he was dating someone who identified as transgender.

His words got to me. And based on my experience with men, I knew how most thought about trans women. Once, I was chatting with a guy on Tinder. It was friendly and sweet, but all of a sudden the conversation took a turn. I told him that he seemed to be looking for a hookup, and I wasn't interested in that. And then he went off.

> What the fuck do you expect? You're trans. You think these niggas out here gonna take you serious? You think we're gonna settle with you, a trans girl? No. All y'all are is a piece of ass. A toy.

At first, I was shocked that someone would talk to me like that. And then, anger and hurt sank in. I realized that what he said probably was true. That he wasn't the only one who thought like that. And it's perceptions like these that prevent many trans men and women from disclosing their identities to new partners. I understand why my trans brothers and sisters might not want to: fear of rejection combined with fear of widespread transphobia and the hate crimes that come along with it. I am up front about my identity, but even still, I've interacted with many men who, after learning that I'm trans, try to blame me for their own attraction to me. And this can quickly become violent.

Josh knew about my identity from the beginning, and he seemed to be okay with it—he just didn't want other people to know. He told me that it was between us, that it wasn't anyone else's business. Of course intimate details between couples should remain private, but this was more than that. I started to feel trapped, like I was forgetting who I was at my core. No one other than my family knew about the truth of my identity, and I didn't stand up for myself out of fear that I would lose him.

In a way, I felt unable to fight. I started to believe the things he told me: that I would never find anyone else, that I wasn't worthy of love. But at the same time, I really did love him. I thought I was going to marry him. And suddenly, just several months into our relationship, things took a turn for the worse.

Chapter 24

MARIZOL

. . . .

On the Fourth of July, my sister invited me to her in-laws' family's house in Long Island for their yearly barbecue. I was excited to go, to spend the day with my sister and my niece and her extended family. I felt comfortable around them. They were always happy and jolly and loving, and I was excited to be away from Josh for a time. The emotional abuse was in full force by this point, and I needed a break, to be around my family, and to enjoy myself.

The house was really nice, in an all-American neighborhood with an in-ground pool. We were all having a good time, sitting outside, eating hot dogs and burgers from the grill. There was sunshine, lots of flowers and trees all over the place. I thought about what had been going on between me and Josh, and I started to come to my senses— anytime I was with my family, away from him, I started to come to my senses. He knew this and tried to further isolate me from them because of it. That day, seeing people around me be happy and functional, celebrating the holiday, I began to realize that things were horrible between us. He wasn't the guy I thought he was.

At the same time, though, I missed him. I wished he was there with me to enjoy this beautiful day.

Out of nowhere, my phone started blowing up. Texts from Josh.

SLUT

FUCK YOU

UR NOTHING BUT A WHORE

And almost immediately, all that clarity I had, all the peace I had been feeling, just went out the door. I didn't understand why he was mad at me, so I tried to contact him. I tried to figure out whatever it was he thought I had done so that I could apologize and make things right.

I texted him:

what's going on?

why are you so mad?

He responded by sending me a link to a pornography website. He had found videos of me.

It was as if he'd punched me. I started to panic, but I tried to keep it to myself. No one in my family knew the truth about our relationship or about my experience with sex work.

Seli noticed that I was distracted. She saw me in the corner, on my phone, desperately calling him over and over.

"I gotta go home," I said.

She looked at me, confused. "Well, we're not leaving now."

"I gotta go now."

"Marizol, we can't leave yet."

For the rest of the party, I was on edge. I couldn't relax. I couldn't enjoy myself. I was so worried that things would be over between us if I didn't get back quick enough.

By the time we were getting ready to leave, it seemed like he had calmed down.

I'm hungry.

Come over.

I want to see you.

I was relieved but still nervous. I made a plate of leftovers for him and said my goodbyes. I felt like I couldn't get back to him fast enough.

MY SISTER dropped me off by the park near his mom's house. It was already dark, but people were still out and walking by, and I waited for him on the corner, across the street from the park.

When he met me, he gestured to a dark area of the park. "Let's go down there," he said.

"Why?"

"There's too many people here."

We walked down the stairs and started talking face-to-face about what had happened. And that's when he started going off on me. Yelling, calling me names. He slapped me across the face, over and over again. He started choking me.

I was crying my ass off, and here he was still beating on me.

"Why are you doing this to me?" It killed me that I was crying hysterically, looking scared and in pain, and he seemed to have no remorse at all. He just kept beating on me. He wanted to know how I could have kept this from him. How could I have lied to him about something like this?

But I didn't lie. I hadn't told him—but I was going to. I just didn't feel ready. I'd only done porn twice, and it was not something I was proud of. It was something I did for survival. I was embarrassed and ashamed, and I didn't want someone to go looking for it, to put it out there for the world to see. I didn't explain this to him in that moment. I couldn't. Instead, I started to think to myself that I was the one in the wrong. That this kind of anger and abuse from him was justified.

At the same time, I felt totally stripped down. Like I had lost myself. I couldn't believe that I had let our relationship come to this. I couldn't believe that I was becoming *that* girl—the one who is abused and too weak to get out. These thoughts made me even more upset and made me feel even more like I was trapped. Like I had nowhere to turn.

Luckily, someone walked by, and I was able to get away. I walked home after the fight, all the way from Manhattan to the Bronx.

The next day, he called me.

"I'm so sorry," he said. "I don't know what happened. I didn't mean it. I swear to God." He was begging me for forgiveness.

I didn't talk to him for maybe four days. He kept calling, kept trying to hit me up. He seemed to return to that charming guy I had fallen in love with, and I fell for it. Things seemed to be okay for a while, but the abuse returned. Over and over again. And with each incident, I felt more and more trapped. More and more like I had lost the me I had fought so hard, and for so many years, for.

I want my trans sisters to be aware of the signs of abuse. Josh isolated me from my friends and family. He made it so that I was wholly dependent on him—financially, socially, emotionally—and forced me to abandon my identity and, essentially, live a closeted life. And that was before he started physically harming me.

We, trans women, need to learn to love and stand up for ourselves. Never should someone tell you to keep your identity secret. Never should someone make you forget who you are. We need to pay attention to the signs, to be brave enough to get out of a relationship when it turns abusive. And though it might at times seem like we won't find anyone who will accept us for who we are, we cannot settle for anything less than what we deserve, which is to love and be loved, just like anyone else.

Chapter 25

SELENIS

. . . .

After that first Christmas home, we didn't see much of Marizol. But it wasn't because she was struggling or because she was hurting. We didn't see Marizol because she was doing well. She was working, living her life. And she was in love. We were all happy for her, relieved that her life had taken on some stability.

I had never met any of Marizol's boyfriends before Josh. Early on in their relationship, she had expressed to me how happy she was. She told me how she had met his family, and how he was very accepting of who she was. This excited me, but I was very cautious. I suppose that I'm not the most trusting of human beings—it takes me time to warm up to others, to let them into the circle. But I tried to reserve judgment. I wanted to be happy for her. I wanted to believe that she was in control of her life.

All right, we'll see, I thought to myself.

But then I met him. And right away, I knew there was something I didn't like.

Before Marizol brought him over, she said to me, "Promise me you'll be nice."

"What? Of course I'll be nice!"

But, when he finally came to my home, my version of nice—the only way I could keep my promise to Marizol—was to not say anything.

From the moment he sat in my living room, I did not like him at all. Physically, I thought that my sister could do much better. She had told me that he was really into martial arts and other athletic activities, and I had imagined this fit, handsome man. In reality, he seemed a bit fluffy to me, different from what I expected. But she was into him, and who was I to judge that?

But more than his physical appearance, I just didn't feel like I could trust him. I've always been an observant person, and I think my experience as an actress has influenced how closely I read others. My mother seemed to like him—he could speak Spanish and was flattering her, saying all of the right things—but I got the vibe of someone who was phony, someone who was trying too hard to impress. I felt like he was trying to sell me something, like he was a used car salesman covering up a shoddy transmission and worn-out brakes. I didn't see any honesty in his eyes. Instead, I saw that he was working this big personality of his—just like Jose Sr.

I remember Marizol sitting on the couch beside him, looking at me. Her eyes were almost pleading for my approval. She had a nervous smile, and she kept looking over to me with anticipation.

But it was awkward. He and Mami were the only ones talking.

Marizol mouthed to me, "Be nice to him!"

And I mouthed back, "I'm not saying anything!"

Oh, Seli, I thought to myself, *stop being such a hard-ass. Your sister's happy! Look at her! She's fawning all over him. And he's telling you that he loves her.*

When we were finally alone, she asked me: "What's wrong? Are you okay?"

"I'm fine," I said, not wanting to upset her.

"What do you think?"

"Oh, I don't know—I just met him!"

Such a lie! Like I've never not had an opinion. So I added: "I did think he'd be cuter."

She laughed it off. "Oh my God, shut up!"

I didn't say anything to her that day because I wanted to be open-minded and supportive. She looked happy and healthy, and so what if I didn't understand what she saw in him? I watched Marizol as she sat on my couch, and I was reminded of how awkward and nervous I felt when I brought my first boyfriend home. I remembered the pride I had; it was like telling everyone in the neighborhood, "Hello, my boyfriend is here!" That day had been so important for me, and so I imagined that it must have been even more important for her, as a trans woman. I didn't want to ruin it. *How evil would that be of me?*

Still, I couldn't get rid of this feeling in my gut that something was terribly wrong. Now, knowing what I know, I wish I had spoken up. But had I been more vocal, she would have shut me out more, and he would have taken more control over her life.

The feeling of concern didn't go away. The more time went on, the more suspicious I became.

One incident sticks out in my mind. Just a short time after our first meeting, Marizol called me because she didn't have money for food. I told her to come over and that I would buy her some groceries. I knew that he had been spending a lot of time over at her place, and my instinct was not to give her money, though I didn't quite know why.

I went shopping, and later they came by. He drove her to my house, they filled his car up with the groceries and left.

I still don't like this guy, I thought. *Like, are you serious? You can't even buy groceries for my sister?*

After that, I didn't see him again. And I barely heard from my sister. I assumed she was doing her own thing, that she was in love and in new relationship bliss. It wasn't until the Fourth of July at my in-laws' place did I realize that something more must have been going on. She was on her phone, and I watched her go from having fun and enjoying herself to nervous and preoccupied in a matter of seconds. Later that night, I dropped her off at his place and from then on I didn't hear from her much. We talked here and there, but for the rest of the summer she was certainly more absent than she was present.

THE WOMEN'S EVENT is an annual gala fundraiser hosted by The Center, an LGBT community center in New York City. In 2013, Laverne Cox was to be one of the event's three honorees, and I was asked to introduce her.

I hadn't thought about it until that moment, but I realized that, though my sister was living her life, she wasn't living her life openly as a trans woman. Instead, it seemed to me that she was trying to live her life as a cis-woman and that part of her was in hiding. I wanted her to be celebrated. I had the idea that, during my speech, I would say publicly and proudly that I had a sister who was trans. I asked Marizol if she'd like to come with me, if she'd be okay with me announcing this to the world.

She seemed so surprised that I wanted to take her. "Me? Really?" I remember the look on her face—it was the same look she gave me that day in the attic, when I asked her if she wanted to be a woman.

"Yes, of course you!"

"Oh my God, yes!"

And almost immediately, her eyes darkened, her smile dropped into a frown.

"Well," she said, "I don't know. I think it will make him mad."

She told me that Josh didn't like her talking about being trans. That he didn't think it was anybody's business or that people should know. I found this unsettling. Disturbing. I thought that he had accepted her for who she was. But instead, she was hidden. I started to see cracks.

"I don't understand," I said.

"I mean, he wouldn't want his mom to find out. Or his friends."

For me, that was the first real indication that something was horribly wrong between them. But I gave her space, let her think about it. She went back and forth a little, but eventually came back to me and said, "You know what? No matter what he says, I'm going to do this."

The night of the Women's Event was magical. I praised Laverne for her fierceness, for her bravery. And I thanked her—I thanked her for showing people all over the world that trans folk were more than just oversexualized stereotypes. I thanked her, again, for giving my sister Marizol a voice.

Laverne, through her amazing, beautiful, honest portrayal of Sophia, has broken many, many barriers. Laverne has created a revolution. People are talking, people are listening. You are educating and it is about damn time we listened. I was drawn to Laverne from day one, for many reasons, not only because she is a goddess, and when she walks into a room she demands attention. She is not only beautiful, she is not only eloquent, she is kind and she is honest, and I love that about her. And Laverne and I have had many many conversations, and she knows exactly why I adore her.

Because you are the face and voice to someone who I love very much. Because I am the proud sister of a transgender woman. And she is here with me tonight and she is sitting at the same table as Miss Laverne Cox. Marizol, my beautiful sister. I have seen firsthand, I have been made witness to how difficult it is to live your truth at times. But Laverne—being recognized tonight and being acknowledged tonight by Hollywood, by the media—Laverne is a revolution. I am so grateful to not only Jenji Kohan and Netflix and Lionsgate for giving this opportunity to this amazing brilliant actress transgender woman to have a voice, and to do it with dignity....What you are doing, my dear friend, is amazing. There are homes all across America, all over the world, that have never uttered the word *transgender* yet are now having conversations about it.

199

When I said that I had a trans sister, the audience broke into applause. By the end of the speech, there wasn't a dry eye in the house. I still get goosebumps thinking about it. And Marizol was working it, kiking with the ladies from *Orange Is the New Black*. Later, we went to an after-party and had the best time. Finally, she was being appreciated and applauded and celebrated. Finally, she wasn't hiding any part of herself.

And then we got home.

Immediately, she was on the phone. The conversation with Josh started out in hushed whispers, but then her voice got louder and louder. I realized that they were in an argument. Suddenly, she was crying. She had planned on sleeping over at my place, but she ended up going home, and I don't know what happened when she got there.

Chapter 26

MARIZOL

. . . .

When my sister spoke about me at the Women's Event, it was the first time my trans identity was made public. Before that night, I didn't really think about the fact that I was living a kind of stealth life. The fact that nobody knew that I was trans, including Josh's family and friends, fed my ego. It made me feel beautiful and confident, and it was refreshing to be seen as a cis-woman.

I've always believed that being trans is only part of my identity. It is a significant part, of course; it has defined how, for much of my life, I've interacted with the world. But first and foremost, I see myself as a woman. Often, when people learn you are trans, they begin to treat you differently. Sometimes it is with judgment, but sometimes it is with curiosity or concern. And always having to explain yourself or educate people on what it means to be trans can be exhausting.

The fact that people didn't know that I was trans meant that they could focus on me, on my personality, and not solely on my trans identity, and this was freeing. At the same time, though, it also made me paranoid. I always worried that, as people got to know me, they would start to analyze my appearance and question me. To this day, I worry that certain aspects of my physical appearance—my height, my broad shoulders—give me away.

There is a stigma in the trans community that being able to pass is something to be celebrated. It is glorified. There is a feeling that, if you can't pass, then you aren't good enough to hang out with the girls who do. But we all come in different shapes and sizes. We all come with particular traits that make us the individuals we are. I am self-conscious about my height, but plenty of cis-women are taller than me! My height doesn't make me any less of a woman.

Unfortunately, this internalized transphobia—especially when combined with the ways many ethnic communities have been social-ized to value whiteness—creates a culture of shame for anyone who falls outside of an impossible standard. And it breaks my heart. We, the trans community, already experience so much discrimination and hate; must we also discriminate against ourselves? Not all of us are born with feminine features. Not all of us can afford surgeries to cor-rect what makes us feel self-conscious. Let's stop putting each other down. Let's celebrate our beautiful differences, and glorify all of us.

When I was dating Josh, the combination of my insecurities and his machismo made it worse for me. He was the man, and I was the woman, and I needed to listen to what he said. I needed to respect him. He didn't want me to dress up nice or to wear makeup because if I had him why did I need to show myself off like that? Now, I realize that he wasn't building me up when he told me that he didn't see me as trans—instead, it was just part of the way he was constantly putting me down. It was just part of how he got me into the palm of his hand.

I was scared when my sister asked me to be a part of her speech. I wanted to go to the event, but I felt so stripped down by my relation-ship. He had taken so much from me, and I knew that I was losing myself. It was hard for me because I really did love him, and despite the abuse and manipulation, I was afraid to lose him. He knew what made me feel good. He knew how I wanted to be loved. It felt good to receive that love, and that's what kept me there, silenced and trapped, for so long.

I chose to go to the awards even though he didn't want anyone else to know the truth about my identity. I felt powerful, like I was finally doing something I wanted to do, not just following his commands.

He was always controlling everything—where I was going, what I was doing, what I was wearing, who I was talking to—and I needed to put my foot down. I needed to say, "This is who I am, and you better be okay with it."

I didn't think that the event was going to be so intense, that I would be able to feel the energy in the room in the way that I did. I sat at one of the main tables with my sister, a few other trans girls, and Laverne Cox. It was thrilling to be sitting right next to this icon who was changing how the world understood what it meant to be transgender. But it was also intimidating! I didn't know how to act or what to say, so I thanked her for all that she'd done for the community. She was welcoming and kind and made me feel accepted and supported.

During her speech, I didn't expect my sister to go into detail about me, or about how, as I transitioned, we went on a journey of self-discovery together. For her to go up there in front of so many people and share her truth with everyone was so powerful for me. I always knew that my sister supported and accepted me, but that night, I felt validated. Loved and seen. I didn't know that she was going to get so emotional, and that made me get emotional, and Laverne and the other trans girls at the table got emotional, too. We were all tearing up, and they reached over and held my hand.

I had the time of my life that night. When Seli revealed the truth about my identity, people were so surprised when they heard the news. All eyes were on me, and the room broke out into cheer. Into celebration. I felt so proud to say, "Yeah, I *am* trans." After all I had been through with Josh, I needed that kind of validation. I gained a sense of confidence. I felt like I was getting the real me back.

He was so upset that I went. He was aggressive and combative. He was trying to control me. I had done something good for myself, and there he was, trying to ruin it. I had felt loved at the event, which I certainly wasn't feeling from him. I said to him, "Damn, you should feel proud. Whenever you do something good for you, I am happy for you. And now I'm doing something good for me for once."

Still, we made up. Our relationship was like a roller coaster. One day might have been bad, but the next day it was good again. And

whenever things turned bad, I was reminded of all of the good moments we'd had, and I kept hoping that things would get better. I kept
thinking that we could get through these hardships and that our relationship would be better because of it.

I KNEW that Josh had never celebrated Christmas like my family did.
He grew up without a father and didn't have much family other than
his brother and his mom. Usually, he'd spend the holidays at home,
playing video games, waiting for his mom to bring him leftovers from a
party she'd gone to at a neighbor's house. He had a lot of anger about
the holidays, and I was sympathetic to his experience and wanted to
help him. I wanted to show him what our holidays were like. I wanted
him to know what it was like to be part of a big family, to really feel
the love in the room. I thought that it could help him understand more
about me and that it would help our relationship.

But nothing went like I'd hoped.

Isa and I were at our parents' house, getting ready, while everyone
was next door at Seli's. Josh called me. He was downstairs, and he
didn't want to go to the party by himself.

"I'm almost finished getting ready," I told him. "Just come up to my
parents' house for a minute."

He rang the bell and I let him up, and out of nowhere, Isa started
getting all antsy.

"Mami and Papi don't like having visitors over while they aren't
here," she said.

"He's not visiting! He just came to get me. I'm almost ready."

"He needs to get the fuck outta here."

Isa is the kind of girl who could go from zero to one hundred real
quick, but I couldn't understand what had set her off. I was trying to
stay calm, to keep everyone on good terms. This was the first time Josh
was going to meet my extended family, and I really wanted it to go
well. But Isa and I weren't really on good terms ourselves. About two
weeks before, she had picked a fight with me over Facetime.

"Oh, so your boyfriend—is he gay?"

"No, he's not gay," I said. "I'm trans, but I'm a trans *woman*. Just because I'm trans doesn't have anything to do with my sexuality, or with his sexuality." This is a common misconception: that men who date trans women must be gay. And this, combined with pervasive homophobia, is just one of the reasons why men like Josh want to keep their partner's true identity hidden. Isa didn't intend something homophobic with her question; I think she was asking me because she really didn't know. I tried to play it safe with her, to keep calm and explain things to her about me, about my identity. But sometimes, with those we feel closest to, it can be difficult to say all that we want to, especially in moments of tension. And God knows that she and I, as close as we were in age, had always fought with one another.

Then, at my parents' house on Christmas, before I knew it, she and Josh started arguing. I was going back and forth between the two of them, trying to calm everything down. But when I tried to console Isa, he became even more angry, and so I went to his side, which then set her off again. In the end, she called him something she knew would set him off: "Faggot!"

They both started screaming. I was so upset—this was not how I pictured the day would go at all! I got in between the two of them and started begging for them to stop—but I didn't want to take anybody's side because I felt that both of them were in the wrong. For Isa, I thought: *How could you deliberately disrespect my guest like this? You know that someone like him has always worried that people would see him as gay. That's why he wanted to keep me being trans a secret. His friends don't know, his mom doesn't even know!*

And as for Josh, I wanted to say: *You are at my parents' house, arguing with my sister—why don't you just stay quiet?*

I couldn't say any of these things, of course. The fighting got so loud and nasty that everyone from next door came over to see what was going on. I was so embarrassed. Tony, who has always defended all of us, stood up to Josh and took Isa's side. Selenis was trying to calm everyone down, to talk it all through.

"Listen," she said. "Let's just start this over again. We got off on the wrong foot. Marizol, you and Josh can still come over. We can pretend that it never happened."

But by this point, I felt like Christmas was ruined.

For so many years afterward, when I'd think about what went down that day and how Isa reacted, I could never understand what went wrong or why things turned out the way they did. I didn't know if Isa was jealous of the fact that I had a boyfriend, or she couldn't accept the fact that I was trans, or she didn't understand why I was with this particular guy. But as time went on, I started to wonder whether she saw what I had been trying so hard to hide. Just as Seli had a bad feeling about Josh from the very first moment she met him, I wonder whether Isa had one as well. Could she sense the abuse or the way that he was stripping me down?

Isa has always reacted to conflict directly. If she doesn't like you, she does not pretend—she makes her feelings known, without any bullshit. It's something I respect about her. But in that moment, I was so overwhelmed, so hurt. I felt like everyone had their own ego to protect, that no one except Seli was thinking about how I was feeling. At that point, I didn't care how Isa felt or how Josh felt. I was trying to keep things cool, and I wanted so badly to stay and start over, but I knew that it would turn into a whole 'nother thing between Josh and me once we got home, so I decided that it was time to leave.

Before we left, I turned to Isa. "You're not my sister," I said. "You're dead to me."

I regretted those words the moment I said them. I didn't mean what I said, of course; I just said it out of anger. I just said it because I was afraid of what was going to happen next. To this day, Isa and I still haven't gotten past this. I realize that, from her perspective, it seemed like I was picking him over her. But it wasn't that. I was trying to cover up the abuse I'd been going through for months and months. I was trying to be on his good side so that I wouldn't be cursed out or hit on when we got home.

The moment we left, I was filled with regret. *I can't do this,* I thought. *I can't leave right now and choose him over my family after all we've been through.* But still, my fear was overwhelming every other emotion swirling inside me. *But if I don't leave, he's gonna really fuck me up.*

We headed back to his mom's house. On the train, he accused me of looking at other guys.

"I just left my family because of you," I said. "I'm not looking at anyone!"

But he wouldn't listen. He cursed me out in front of everyone and then went and sat on the other side of the train, as far away from me as he could. I thought about getting off and going back to my parents' house. I thought about just leaving him right there. But he was living with me, and I didn't know how to get rid of him.

For the next few days, between Christmas and New Year's, things were fine between us. But I was on edge, ready for another fight to break out. I remember my sister contacting me to come over for New Year's Eve, but I knew I couldn't go. I was trapped. Josh made me feel like I had to be with him that night, like I had to once again choose him over my family. But I was also so embarrassed about what had happened, about how the whole family had witnessed this massive fight, and I didn't feel ready to confront Isa. To be on the safe side, to protect myself from any kind of fight that might break out between Josh and me, I had to stay with him. And I did, and I was so sad to be apart from my family once again. I thought about the year before, how I was on the right track with my life, how I felt like I was going places. And then I met him, and though I fell madly in love and was in a kind of relationship I never thought I could be in, my life had fallen apart.

I stayed with him that night, but what happened over the next few months was constant fighting, further isolation from my family, and further abuse from Josh.

"Why didn't you defend me?" he'd say.

"What are you talking about? I left with you! Over my family, I chose you!"

During these fights, I tried to make him see the significance of the sacrifice I made for him. But still, I defended Tony and Isa. They were only doing what we all would do: stand up for our family, protect those we love most.

MY SISTER

And then, out of nowhere, he stopped talking to me. He wouldn't respond to my messages or any of my calls. And though his things were still at my apartment, he just disappeared from my life. He had ghosted me like this in the past, which always worried me. I'd think that maybe something terrible had happened to him, that he had relapsed or been in an accident or something worse. And then I'd turn the blame on myself. I'd think about what I had done wrong, about what I had done to make him leave.

But this time, after two weeks of silence from him, I decided that enough was enough. It was almost my birthday, and I wanted to have a good time. I thought about the Marizol I used to be: the bubbly, free-spirited person. And I wanted that girl back.

I went out with my girls, and I started feeling good about myself again. Like I'd finally put myself first, over him. It was then, of course, that he finally called.

"Hey, happy birthday," he said.

I was in shock. Who the fuck did he think he was? At the same time, I was happy to hear from him. I was happy to know that he remembered my birthday.

"I'm about to pull up. Can we talk?"

He didn't want to come inside, so I went out to his car. He said he had told his mom the truth about me, that he wanted to get back together, that he wanted to make things right.

"Look," I said. "I feel like I've been going through a lot with you. You put your hands on me, you put me through a lot of shit."

"Don't bring that up. I'm not happy I did that."

"If you can't deal with this, me and you, you can just go. Please. Let's just break up, and you can go your way and I can go mine."

I was getting my power back, and he didn't like it. He was feeling like his manhood was being threatened, so he threatened me. He wanted me to come crawling back like I always had in the past. He raised his hand, and I flinched. He realized it and caught himself.

"See, this is what I mean. This is why I can't get back with you. This is why I can't deal with your shit. I treated you with kindness and respect, and I am scared of you. If you want to get back together, we're gonna have to start over. You're gonna have to prove to me that this is what you really want. You're gonna have to show me that you love me."

"Why do we have to go through all that? Just take me back now."

"You're not listening to me," I said. "I'm afraid of you. You need to prove yourself to me so that I feel safe around you, so that I can trust you."

Outside of the car, it was pouring rain. Water was rushing like a little river. I moved to get my umbrella ready, to get out of the car and leave.

"Be prepared for tomorrow," he said. "'Cuz I'm gonna be calling your sister. I'm gonna be calling your mother. I'm gonna be calling *everybody*, telling them about how you're a whore."

I couldn't believe he'd threaten to betray me in such a way. But I also didn't think he'd actually ever do it.

"That's so fucked up," I said. "You would never."

He didn't say anything in response.

I got out of the car, and as I made my way to the sidewalk, my heel got stuck in the mud and I got soaked.

The next morning, I found out that he had done it: he'd contacted my family, asking them for money I "owed" him and told them that I'd done sex work and that I was a whore. He threatened them and said that they needed to pay him back.

I couldn't believe it. I couldn't believe this person I had loved and cared for could have done something so terrible to me. I thought about how many beautiful moments we had had together, about the feeling of love I'd never ever felt with anyone else.

My heart was in my throat. My heart was in pain for days, weeks, months. I became so depressed, but I still tried to take care of myself. Over the next few months, I spent a lot of time at my parents', just trying to stay level-headed and focused. I thought about all of the things I could do now that I wasn't wasting my time on him, like go back to school or get my GED. But I was heartbroken, and I started to let myself go.

Chapter 27

SELENIS

. . . .

If I had thought Marizol's boyfriend was scum before, what happened on her birthday solidified all of the assumptions I had about him.

That day, he sent me a string of horrible texts.

You think your sister is so innocent,
but you have no idea the kind of shit she's done.

He started to reveal all of these things about Marizol she had told him in confidence. The sex work. The porn. It was the first time I had ever heard those things, and it felt really awful. It felt awful to hear it spoken out loud. I had always suspected that she had been involved in that world at some point or another, but I didn't know to what degree, and I never wanted to be fully aware of the specifics. I never approached Marizol about it because it was her life, and I knew that she needed to make a living. And to be honest, I really didn't want to know. When I got those texts from him, it felt like such a violation of her humanity. She had shared this information with him in confidence, with him as a person she thought she could trust and confide in. And yet here he was, telling the people she loved the most just to hurt her.

Another text came:

> She borrowed money from me,
> and somebody better pay me back.

I never responded to him. I thought to myself, *Go on. Keep sending me whatever you are going to send me, because I am going to use this as evidence against your ass.*

Then, he contacted my mother. I don't know exactly what he told her, but I can assume it was the same. My mother was disturbed by the things he said and refused to repeat them.

What she did tell me was that he asked her for money as well.

"I don't know what to tell you," Mami had replied. "You can come here, but no one is going to give you anything." My mother is always poised and calm. She never would have let him know how shocked or mortified she was by his words.

Of course, he never showed up. He must have known that his threats wouldn't work on us, but he betrayed Marizol anyway. What a cowardly, untrustworthy person. I had been right about him all along.

A few months prior, right after that big fight on Christmas Eve, I remember looking at Marizol and thinking, *Wow, he's really got to you. After all these years you've been away from the family, you are going to choose him?* In truth, I didn't understand the extent of the abuse and manipulation until I received those texts, until he threatened my family. I didn't understand how terrified Marizol was of him.

When I confronted her about him after he sent us those messages, she was very upset. But more than upset, she was overwhelmed with fear. I said to her, "You have to go to the police. You have to file an order of protection."

But she refused.

I was furious. "You can never, ever go back to him." It was like the ultimatum I had given her so many years prior, when I dropped her off at the shelter. "I will not do this again. I will not pick you up from this place that he's left you again—and now, it's even worse because he's involved your family!" I know it seems harsh, but I meant every word I said. If she went back to him, I was prepared to stay out of her life for good.

A WHILE AFTER that, Marizol disappeared from our lives. This broke my heart, but I felt for her, especially after she told me they had broken up. I was glad that monster was finally out of her life, and we kept in touch—calling or texting almost every day—just to check in with each other.

And then, one day over the summer, the communication stopped. I called her, and my calls went straight to voice mail. I texted, but got no response. I couldn't get in touch with her that day, and I couldn't sleep that night.

The next morning, I had this horrible feeling of dread, like a cold shiver that moved up and down my spine telling me that something was horribly, horribly wrong. Something in my gut told me to go to her apartment, but I was terrified of what I was going to find. *What if I find my sister dead?*

I called my sister-in-law Melodie and told her what was going on.

"I need to go over there," I said.

"You can't go by yourself! Wait for me—I'll go with you."

After a short while, I called my brother Tony, and he was even more insistent that Melodie and I couldn't go by ourselves. He was getting out of work soon, and he would take us.

But so much time passed. First, I had to wait for Melodie. Then, for Tony. *What if she needed us, and now it's too late?* I was panicking. I was shaking. I kept calling her phone over and over again—and every time, I got her voice mail. Finally, the three of us drove to her apartment in silence. I think we all had the same fears, but we were too afraid to say them out loud.

Melodie stayed in the car, and Tony and I went up to the building. When we got to the door and reached for the buzzer, a guy with a hood pulled up over his head let us in. I stopped and tried to get a look at his face, but he was going out of his way to hide. Tony told him thanks, and the guy just looked to the ground, pulled the hood down further, and left the building.

"Was that him?" I asked Tony. "I think that was him."

"You think so?"

"I think it was."

When we got to Marizol's door, I knocked. No answer. I knocked again. And again. And then we heard the sound of someone walking on top of broken glass. Tony and I looked at each other.

Finally, we heard her voice. "Who is it?"

"It's Seli," I said. "Open the door."

"Okay," she said, her voice startled. "You just have to give me some time. Hold on."

Tony looked at me. "I'm going back downstairs to see if he's there."

"All right," I said, and I waited outside her door.

After about two minutes, I knocked again. "Marizol, you have to open the door."

She did, just a crack, just enough so that I could see the state she was in. She was completely disheveled, with dark circles under her eyes. She was thin, deflated. She looked tired. She looked battered.

"Did he just leave?" I asked.

"Yeah."

I knew it. I was so angry. "I need to come in."

She stepped to the side and I saw what else he had done.

The apartment was totaled. Completely trashed. From where I stood and what I could see—in the kitchen, down the hall, in the living room—there was not one single corner of the apartment that did not look like a tornado had hit it. There were holes in the walls. Doors pulled from hinges. The paneling around the windows was barely hanging on. Someone had gone completely nuts in there, destroying everything in his path like a hurricane.

My sister did not live like this. She took care of her apartment. She took pride in where she lived. I saw her little trinkets and decorations shattered across the floor. I remember feeling so uncomfortable in there, like a sense of darkness overtook my whole body. I finally had confirmation about all that I suspected about him: that he was a monster, that he couldn't be trusted, that he was dishonest and sneaky and conniving and deceitful. Worst of all, I had confirmation of what I had always feared, but never said out loud: that he had gotten physical, that he had been abusing her. *If he comes back now*, I thought, *this is going to end tragically*. Now, I realize that God had kept me waiting to go over there for a reason. Because if I would have found him there, I would not have been able to control myself.

"Marizol, what happened? I've been trying to call you."

She was hesitant to respond. "He broke my phone," she cried.

"How long has this been going on?"

Getting answers was like pulling teeth.

"A while," she said eventually.

"You look awful."

"Yeah, well, he didn't let me sleep last night. He kept me up fighting."

Oh my God, I thought. *I'm gonna kill him.*

I told her that if she ever put herself in this situation again, if she ever let him back, that I would be done. In retrospect, I know this wasn't the right way to handle it. I had said this exact same thing to her just a few months before, and she kept a lot from me because of it. I didn't mean to punish her for being abused or to further isolate her from the people who could have helped her out of it. Now I see that, in reality, I was just making things easier for him by pushing her away. I wish that I would have just said to her: "I don't agree with this relationship, but I love you and I'm here for you no matter what." But at the time, I was so angry with him. I just wanted her to be safe. And I wanted to be sure that he was out of her life. For good.

In the next few months, things seemed to get better for her, at least superficially. She didn't mention anything about him, and when I'd ask her directly if she'd heard from him, she'd say no. I assumed things were better simply because he was out of the picture.

But I couldn't help but notice a physical change in Marizol. She was falling into a depression, losing weight. Dark circles hung below her eyes, and she didn't put any time or effort into her look. When I saw her, she wasn't her outgoing, happy self. But I know what a breakup can do to a person. I know what it's like to mourn the absence of someone in your life you loved. So, I didn't think much of it.

Little did I know that all of her old demons were coming back to haunt her.

Chapter 28

MARIZOL

· · · · · · · · · · ·

After Josh left, I heard a knock at my door. Was it him coming back? Was it a neighbor, who must have heard us fighting all night? I didn't respond, hoping that whoever it was would just go away.

But then the knock came again. And again.

I tried to walk to the door to look through the peephole, but the result of our fight—the broken glass, knocked-over furniture, plaster from the holes that he'd made in the walls—made it so that I couldn't be as quiet as I'd have liked.

And then I heard her voice: "It's Seli."

Oh my God, I thought. I couldn't have her see my apartment like this. I couldn't let her see *me* like this! What was I going to say?

"Marizol, you have to open up."

"It's not a good time," I said.

"I'm not leaving," she said.

I had no choice but to open the door. There was Seli, standing next to my brother Tony. And they saw it all. I was so embarrassed. I was so ashamed. After Josh had threatened my family on my birthday, Seli told me that I needed to be done with him for good. And I was—but in the past few weeks, we had been talking once again, seeing each other on occasion. I had kept this all from her, of course, knowing that she wouldn't approve, and then he and I had this big fight, my

216

apartment was trashed, and now Seli was here, seeing it all firsthand. I was relieved Josh had left when he did. Not because I wanted to protect him anymore—I was finally done with that—but because I feared, if Seli and Tony had found him there, no one would have been able to control themselves. The physical fight that had transpired between him and me would have then included my brother and sister, too. And who knows what would have happened.

AFTER THAT incident, I went through a dark time. Once again, I found myself alone, lost and in a deep depression. It was like I had gone back in time to the period before I transitioned, when I didn't have a stable place to live, when I was away from my family, when I was struggling with demons that would never leave me alone. It was like my time at Ali Forney never happened. All that I had accomplished, all that I had learned had just disappeared, like I had dreamed it all. I stopped eating. I stopped caring. For months, all I did was sleep and smoke weed. I saw my sister on occasion, and she could tell that something was wrong, but I didn't tell her what I was struggling with. I was drifting through life high, trying to bury all of these memories and feelings that had been building up inside of me for so many years. Whenever they came to mind, I took another hit. And for a short time, until it wore off and I needed more, I felt good. I felt numb.

No one knew what I was going through or what I was thinking about. I was completely alone. In fact, I didn't tell anyone until we began working on this book. What I did do, though, was ask Mami if she had Jose Sr.'s information.

She didn't. I called Seli and asked her if she knew how I could get in touch with him. And she didn't, either.

I remembered how, when I was growing up, he'd call Mami and Papi's house. How I would look at the caller ID, see his number, and hang up the phone. Those calls continued through the years, up until I was sixteen or seventeen, when I was discovering my community and who I was. Whenever I saw that name, or the long number that must have been the number of the prison in the DR, I was reminded of what had happened to me when I was forced to leave Mami and Papi's and live with Jose Sr. and Ruth and Yvette. I tried, for so much of my life, to erase those memories, to block those images from my mind. Images of a dark bedroom. Images of being forced to spend the mornings in the bed with Jose Sr. while my two-year-old sister was left unattended in the living room. Of him trying to hug me and kiss me and me trying to get away but being locked down by his legs. Of him not letting me get up for the whole day. Of him forcing me to do things that, as a little kid, I didn't understand. Things that made me uncomfortable and afraid and angry. And so when he would call, and these memories would return, I remember being overcome by such a feeling of anger that I tried whatever I could to make myself forget.

But no matter how much I tried to bury it, part of it was always there, eating away at me. When I was in my relationship with Josh, and he would tell me that no one else would love me, that no one would accept me for who I am, I believed him. He made me feel small. He made me feel like I wasn't worthy of being loved. And the emotional, physical, and sexual abuse he subjected me to triggered a lot of memories about my biological father. Whenever I was reminded of Jose Sr., or whenever my thoughts drifted to him, I remember thinking, *Why are you coming up in my mind now?* I continued to bury it, trying to pay no mind to the mound that was growing taller and taller until it was impossible to ignore. It wasn't until later that I put these pieces together and saw a pattern in how these two men treated me.

So many times, I thought that it must have been my fault. That I must have done something to deserve all that had happened to me as a little kid, as a young woman. At one point, I remember thinking: *Why is this all happening to me? Why did God choose me? What did I do? Why do I have to live this life? Why do I have to be transgender?* It was all so difficult to deal with. Discovering my gender identity was one thing, and it was something I was able to overcome. But being molested by my own father was another. I decided to focus only on discovering my gender identity; it was something that would enrich my life, something that would make me happy. And it did. But still, part of me couldn't forget the dark memories that haunted me. And as much as I tried not to confront them, I think that they were the cause of much sadness in my life.

After the incident at my apartment, I started to process everything—the downward spiral I fell into after being in such a good place, the abuse, the isolation from my family—and all of those memories came rushing back. I realized, then, how much I had missed having Papi in my life. Papi, who had always been there for me. Papi, who never abused me, who never ever put his hands on me. I thought about my transition, how I had to essentially relearn how to live in the world as a trans woman—and how I wished that Papi had been there to give me advice, to guide me toward the right path.

For so much of my life, part of me has felt almost programmed to duplicate the traditional roles I saw Mami and Papi carry out in our household. Their relationship was full of love, compassion, and support, and they served as an example for how I wanted my relationships to be. Papi was the working man who provided for our family, and he was also present, wanting the best for us. He was there when we needed him most. I wanted to find a man who could care for me in the same ways that Papi did, and I wanted Papi to give me advice like he had given my sisters. I wanted him to tell me to pick a good man, a man who wouldn't put his hands on me. I wanted him to reassure me, to make me feel protected and safe and loved. I wished that he had been there before all of this mess with Josh had happened.

I no longer feel that my relationships need to fulfill these roles. In fact, I now recognize how dangerous the ideal of this traditional structure was to me as a trans woman. Because I wanted to feel cared for and provided for by my man, I was able to write off moments of abuse and control as love and support. When Josh demanded I stop working, for example, he told me that he wanted to take care of me, that he didn't want his girl to have to work. Now I see it for the abuse that it was; though I had my doubts at the time, I was willing to let myself do whatever he thought was best, even if it meant losing part of myself in the process.

At the same time, for many years, I couldn't help but think that the traditional family structure—and the love and support it can provide—didn't apply to me because I was trans or that I, for some reason, didn't deserve to be a part of it. Growing up, I always watched how my brothers and dad protected my sisters, defending them against boyfriends and men. My brothers defended me when I was picked on, of course, but I couldn't help but think: *What if it had been Isa or Seli? What if one of my sisters had been in the kind of relationship I had been in, one where they were abused?* The men in our family would have been livid. Papi would have told my sisters that they were better than that. And Tony and Tito would have stood up for them, maybe even fought for them. But what about me? No one knew about the abuse, of course. But every time Josh put his hands on me, or emotionally manipulated me, I almost felt like I wasn't validated as a woman. That part of him knew that he could get away with it because I wasn't protected in the same way that cis-women are.

I don't blame Papi or my brothers for not standing up for me in the same way they stood up for my sisters. All of us struggled, for so many years, to understand what it was that I was going through and who I was. As my sister has said: we didn't have the language, we didn't have the education. I can only hope that things will be different for my young trans brothers and sisters.

My relationship with Josh helped me realize my worth. It helped me realize that I don't need to put up with violence or abuse just so that I can fulfill someone else's expectations of who I need to be. Family structures or romantic relationships in the LGBTQ+ community might not look like traditional ones, but we have the right to create relationships that are meaningful. We all deserve to be defended. We all deserve to be accepted and loved and cared for.

Chapter 29

SELENIS & MARIZOL

. . . .

Once I finally had enough stability to move out of that dark, stuffy home next door to my parents' house, I looked for another apartment. It would be only my daughter, Alina, and me—my marriage was finally over, and I couldn't wait to start my new life in my own space, paying my own bills, taking care of myself.

This one building in particular had caught my eye for months. It was a new construction in Riverdale, and whenever I drove past it, I thought, *This would be a great place to live*. When I finally was able to begin my search, I went straight over. And they showed me a unit that I loved. It was a corner penthouse apartment with a huge terrace. There was so much sunlight streaming through the big, open windows, I never needed to turn on the lights. What a difference from all those years I'd lived in suffocating darkness.

New Year's was coming up, and I wanted to celebrate and say goodbye to my past life. I had the terrace, and a nice firepit, and I decided to throw a party with those I loved most, just Alina and me, Mami and Papi, my brothers and their families, Isa, Marizol, and my close friend Rosal and her parents. We were going to write, on little slips of paper, all that we wanted to leave behind.

We were going to throw all these negative emotions and experiences into the fire and watch them burn.

. . . .

ON NEW Year's Eve, Selenis invited me over to her place in Riverdale. I didn't want to go. I wasn't ready to face everyone after all that had happened. But she insisted. She had a plan for us all to burn all that we had been holding on to and wanted to get rid of in our lives.

I had so much that I wanted to burn away. I was haunted by memories of my biological father, by my ex, and I had lost myself. I had entered a deep depression. I wasn't taking care of myself. I had let myself go. It took a lot of effort to get myself together to attend that New Year's Eve party. I tried as best I could, but I had gotten a cold, and I was feeling awful.

"Oh my God," Selenis said when I arrived. "Look at you! You have to take care of yourself."

She touched my forehead. I was burning up.

"You have to go to the doctor!"

My cough was bad. I was a mess.

But when I walked inside, the energy in the apartment was fresh and bright. Everyone was excited to see me. My nieces and nephew were happy to be with me. I thought that burning away my demons could be a wake-up call for me to get out of the depression I was in and to leave everything behind that had happened over the past year.

. . . .

I REMEMBER LOOKING around at everyone, slips of paper in their hands, and thinking, *This is a big moment for everyone here.* I knew for Marizol that it was a big moment, though I didn't know exactly what she was going through. For myself, I knew that this moment was huge. My career had completely turned around. I was in the second season of *Orange Is the New Black* and had recently learned that I was going to be a series regular in the upcoming season. But I still wanted to get rid of the fears and anxieties that had haunted me for years.

A lackluster career. No money in the bank. Starving artist. A failed marriage. Guilt of not being in a marriage like my parents'. Those were the things I wrote down on my slip.

· · · ·

I **WROTE** down all the reasons why I was depressed: My experience with my biological dad. My experience with my ex. Forgetting the Marizol I had fought so hard for.

I wanted to have peace. To forgive those who hurt me and caused me pain. I was ready to move on.

· · · ·

WE WERE GOING to leave all of that behind. And everyone took it so seriously, staring into the firepit, watching to make sure that their slips of paper and all they had been hanging on to turned to ash.

"Bye, Felicia!" we all started to yell and cheer.

It felt really good. I felt powerful. It was the first time in a long time I felt good about what was coming. It was almost as if it was all worth it, all those years of struggling, being unhappy. I wasn't on antidepressants anymore, and it felt good to look around at my new place and think, *I did this*.

Once all the celebrating calmed down and a silence took over, Rosal's dad asked, "Who's Felicia?"

And we all burst into laughter.

Chapter 30

MARIZOL & SELENIS

. . . .

After the New Year's celebration at my sister's house, I was supposed to go out with my friend. But when I got to her house, I felt so sick, I went straight to bed. I spent the whole night, in the clothes I had been wearing, shivering under a sheet.

I woke up the next morning soaked. My friend had come back home, and I was embarrassed for her to see me in such a way. She didn't know about my depression either, and I felt vulnerable and exposed. She was really worried and encouraged me to go to the hospital. I didn't want anyone else to see me that way, like my sister or my parents, so I called an ambulance and was taken to the ER by myself.

My cold had turned into pneumonia, and one of my lungs wasn't functioning properly. The doctors hooked me up to a breathing machine and admitted me to intensive care. I was so scared; I couldn't believe that I had let myself get so low. I couldn't believe how numb I had been to all of it. I felt like I couldn't breathe, and I started to panic. That's when I had to call Seli, and she came rushing with my parents.

It was then that I had to sign a form saying that, if I was unconscious and could no longer speak, Seli would be the one to make decisions about my care. *How could I have let this happen?* I was afraid that I was literally going to lose my life.

On my second day in the hospital, Seli said that she wanted to go by my apartment to pick up a few things.

"No," I said. "You can't."

"What do you mean?" she asked.

"It's kinda messy."

"Girl, I don't care!"

"No. I don't think you should."

I couldn't let her go there. My apartment was trashed. And when I say "trashed," I mean it. Piles of trash everywhere. There were roaches, mice. You had to climb over it all to move down the kitchen, to get to the bathroom. I had fallen into such a dark place that I didn't even care.

"Well," Seli said, "someone has to go."

Finally, I agreed that Seli's ex-husband and Papi would be the ones to go, but I was so embarrassed.

And that's when the floodgates opened. I told Seli about everything that had happened. I told her about the abuse in my relationship, about how worthless I felt. I told her how I thought that no one would love me. And, like always, she was there for me, listening.

Everything in my apartment had to be thrown out. My former brother-in-law told Seli that it looked like the apartment of someone who had given up. It looked like the apartment of someone who had decided they didn't care if they went on living.

. . . .

IN THE HOSPITAL, Marizol opened up to me about what she'd been going through. It wasn't until years later, however, when we began writing this book, that she finally divulged what had happened to her when she was just a small child.

When she finally told me, I couldn't help but think of two particular moments. One was the day she called me, almost in a panic, asking if I had Jose Sr.'s number. Something in her voice, something startling, made me feel immediately sick, but I couldn't put it into words.

The other moment was years before, when she was just a teenager. I had asked her if anyone had ever hurt her or touched her or violated her in any way. You might be wondering: What prompted me to ask such a question, seemingly out of the blue? And the answer is because I have always had a connection with my sister. I know when something is wrong—like that day I couldn't get in touch with her, only to find her and her apartment in shambles. It's like an alarm goes off in my soul.

When I asked her this question, I think that part of me knew the answer, but I never could have imagined that it happened when she was so young, so innocent. Maybe because I was too young then myself to understand that people are capable of acting in such a foul way. Maybe because, in a million years, I never would have thought that someone could do that to a baby, let alone to their own baby. I had assumed, during the time Marizol was taken away from us, that her biological parents had spanked her, that they were mean, that they were unloving. But nothing more. Nothing like the nightmare that had really taken place. And I know my parents never could have imagined it either.

I hate that we didn't know. I hate that man for doing what he did. At times, I also hate Ruth for being unable to protect her child. But my anger really lies with the foster care agency and with the broken system that handed over a young, innocent child to addicts it was unable to supervise. Not once did the agency follow up to look after her. I doubt that they ever really knew where she was or with whom.

For years, Marizol had lived with us, and it wasn't through the system. It was because Ruth's mother had called us and begged us to take her home.

. . . .

I WAS in the hospital for nearly a week, but I made a full recovery. Most people don't get out of that kind of situation, and I felt so grateful, so lucky to have been given a second chance. I thought, *God must have something in store for me. There must be a reason why I am still living.* For the first time in a very long time, I had hope.

For a few weeks, I stayed with Mami and Papi while my apartment was exterminated and repainted. When I finally returned to my place, now clean and empty, I felt like I had a fresh start on life. I remembered what it was like to be homeless, and I was so thankful that I still had a place to call my own. I got new furniture, hung pictures on the walls. I wanted to reclaim this space for my own, to have it reflect me. And I began to come to terms with all the pain I had suffered; I started to learn how to cope with it.

It wasn't easy. The next few years were a struggle. I had my good days, but the memories and feelings would always come back. Sometimes, the smallest thing would trigger me, threatening to push me back into that awful depression. Sometimes, all I wanted was to go hit that blunt just so I could forget. It was a challenge not to. I'd go from hurt to angry to sad, and then the cycle would start all over again. But there was a light at the end of the tunnel.

My sister and the rest of my family helped me get back on my feet. I started cooking again. I came out of my depression. I started to work through my past through therapy. And I, once again, started to live my life for me—for *Marizol*. What kept me going was reflecting upon all that I'd been through—being bullied at school, taking the money, transitioning, moving into Ali Forney, falling into an abusive relationship—and how it almost ended my life. I knew I could never end up back in that depressive state again. I knew that I didn't want my parents, my sister, my siblings, my nieces and nephew to have to bury me. And I knew that I didn't want my trans brothers and sisters to fall into the same situations that I had.

. . . .

SHORTLY AFTER MARIZOL was back in her apartment and working on healing emotionally, the Stonewall Foundation contacted me. They wanted to present Marizol and me with a Vision Award. I was so excited to share the news with my sister.

"They want to honor us both," I told her.

"But why me?" Marizol asked.

"Why you?! Because it takes courage to live your truth!"

Upon hearing this, her face lit up. I was thrilled to see, after all we'd been through, her big, beautiful, infectious smile.

"OH MY GOD, SIS!" she giggled. "This is crazy!"

I smiled but shook my head. "No, it's not crazy—you deserve this!"

Finally, it was a moment of light and celebration.

· · · ·

I'D ALWAYS thought that activists were people who protested or went to rallies. People who lobbied Congress for change. It wasn't until I was at the awards ceremony with my parents that I realized what telling my story to others could do. By speaking out about my experiences, maybe others who'd been through similar struggles wouldn't feel so alone. I'm so inspired by the work of other activists who tell their stories boldly and proudly, who take a stand against discrimination and hate. I wanted to continue to make progress in this tradition, not only for the trans community and the LGBTQ+ community but also for all of humanity. I knew how valuable it was to have my family supporting me, and I wanted to help others feel supported, too. And because my sister already had a platform, I felt like I had to take advantage of that privilege. There was no way I could not.

So, I became vocal about my experience as a trans woman of color, educating and informing others, being a supportive voice for the next generation of trans men and women. I spoke about my story to magazines like *Cosmo Latina* and *People en Español*. Selenis and I were recognized at the 2016 Anti-Violence Project Courage Awards. For Pride Week, I had a cooking segment on Telemundo's *Adictivo TV*. And I was invited, by myself, to speak about bullying and domestic violence at an event organized by the Office of the Bronx Borough President. With each event, I was sure to bring Mami and Papi with me. It was important to have them there because they knew all that I had been through. Having them there made me feel like I was accomplishing something, like I was finally doing something with my life that would make them proud.

I was making myself proud, too. Despite all that had happened to me, I was moving in the right direction. I was living my truth. After years of hiding, of losing myself, I was finally being validated and seen.

And I realized I could find my strength by helping others—so that they could be validated and seen, too.

EPILOGUE

. . . .

Dear Readers,

To say it's been hard to write this book doesn't describe the half of it—but I also know that it's been the most important thing I've ever done. I never would have thought I would be writing a book with my sister! I am so honored and humbled to have had this opportunity to share our story together.

In many ways, writing our story has been a form of therapy. It has made me realize so much about myself, and I feel like I have grown as a woman because of it. Writing this book has helped me to stop running from my problems and to confront them head-on. I have been able to finally begin the process of healing because of it.

But healing is not pretty.

Whenever you begin to heal, you need to know that it's going to be hard. Sometimes, you need to first tear open your wounds to remove whatever is causing you pain. It's been a roller coaster, and I've had my moments. And not just me but my sister, too. Together, we've had to directly face the past and all that has happened to us on this journey. I feel so close to my sister, and so grateful for her love and support throughout these years. I'm proud to stand next to her as an activist, as a friend, as a sister.

We wrote this book because we wanted to heal but also because we knew that so many people go through experiences like ours. We know that so many people feel like they have to suffer on their own, like I once did. We hope our story proves otherwise. We hope that it shows the world that, regardless of how we identify, we are all humans. That we all go through trauma and hurt. We don't need to suffer alone.

Furthermore, as a member of the LGBTQ+ community, I think it is my responsibility to lift others up and show support. And I hope this book inspires others to do the same. We already take so much shit from society—we shouldn't be putting each other down. Let's be proud of who we are. Let's show up for each other, be each other's community. Let's show the world that we all can overcome. That we all can rise.

I've made many mistakes. And I hope that by reading my story you never have to feel like you need to make the same mistakes I made. I'm not saying you shouldn't make any mistakes—we all need to mess up from time to time to learn and grow. My experiences and mistakes have led me to the place where I am today, and I feel stronger and more resilient because of them.

Still, at times I wish I could speak to my younger self. Tell her that she is worth it. That she is loved. That she should make better choices. That she should be confident, believe in herself and her abilities, and just go for it, whatever "it" may be. I wish I could tell my younger self, "It was never your fault."

Sometimes, life deals you a hand that forces you to make a choice: you can either fight for survival, or you can let yourself weep life away. I choose to fight. As much pain and hurt as I've experienced and as weak as I've been, I've somehow always managed to get back on my feet and fight back. I never wanted to end up like my biological mother. I never wanted to become a statistic. I never wanted to become a victim. I wanted to make my family proud, to have them look at me and think, *Wow, she's become something.*

To my readers who are transgender, I hope this book gives you the tools and resources you need not only to survive but also to thrive. I hope that it will help my trans brothers and sisters embrace their truth, love and accept themselves for who they are. To my readers who are not transgender or who are outside of the LGBTQ+ community, I hope that this book gives you the opportunity to put yourself in someone else's shoes. I hope that it helps you look outside of the box, educate yourself on what it means for someone to be born different from you. We, transgender folk and the greater LGBTQ+ community, have been on this earth just as long as everyone else—and we aren't going anywhere.

MY SISTER has always been supportive of me, and I have been attached to her since that first day I arrived at Mami and Papi's house. She's my best friend, my mentor. She's always there for me, no matter what. For several years, however, I did not have a relationship with the rest of my family. During that time, I learned what it's like to spend holidays alone. I learned what it's like to not have that foundation of support. But I've also learned what it's like to rebuild those relationships, no matter how daunting it might seem.

Now, I am blessed to have the rest of my family in my life again; but I also know that this is not the reality for many of my trans brothers and sisters. We live in a cruel world, one where it can feel like everyone is against us. And many of us get to a point where we feel like we aren't wanted by anyone at all. This is why family support for the trans community is so important. My sister and I wrote this book to show that, no matter how difficult it might seem, or how scary it might be, it is possible to transition and keep your family close. We wrote this book to show that transitioning doesn't have to be done alone. We wrote this book to show that it's a process that the whole family can take on. It's not an easy process by any means. It's normal for family members of trans folk to feel confused, to feel a loss, to experience many conflicting emotions all at once. But we also hope that you will do your best to try to understand your loved one. To put your judgments and preconceived understandings about the world aside. Love is love.

Now, AFTER years of struggle, I can proudly say: I know there's a future for me. Participating in the creative arts—whether it be modeling, makeup and hair styling, or writing this book—feeds my soul. It gives me the chance to escape, to feel free, to leave all my doubts behind and believe in myself. I know I have the potential to do so much in this world, from continuing to work as an activist to pursuing my interests in acting and modeling, to eventually living my dream and having my own cooking show. I want to be able to use my platform, whatever it may be, to continue to educate and bring awareness to others about what it means to be transgender. I share my story, not just for myself, but for my trans brothers and sisters who are struggling, who are experiencing discrimination and hate. I share my story so that others know that they are not alone. I share my story to acknowledge and celebrate the fact that I am a part of a community of transgender survivors. We have so much to give. We have so much to offer. And so I fight. I fight so that one day, we can shine. And I am grateful to know that no matter what happens, I have someone in my corner: my sister.

Marizol Leyva

ACKNOWLEDGMENTS

From Selenis

Back in July 2015, Caitlyn Jenner appeared on the cover of *Vanity Fair*. I was thrilled to see her celebrated after what I can only imagine were years of intense inner struggle. The next day, however, I woke up with a different feeling. I asked myself: *What is it about that article and cover that is now making me feel so unsettled?* I realized that the reason was because of my sister Marizol and the countless other trans folk I'd met throughout the years. People unable to afford surgeries if they wanted them. People without access to hormones and qualified, caring doctors. People without glamour teams and designers at their beck and call. And especially, people with no opportunity to grace the cover of an influential magazine. I realized that this kind of representation, while positive for Caitlyn, was dangerous for those without the resources: what happens to those trans folk who don't fall into this specific category of glamorous, rich, and famous? The decision to write this book came from a place of wanting to share a realistic account of what it means to be transgender—specifically, what it means to be a transgender person of color of modest means. I am indebted to those who helped make this story heard.

To my parents, who have always been incredibly supportive of all of us. There are no words to express how much they are loved and appreciated. To my daughter, Alina, who from day one has filled my life with more joy than I ever thought possible. To my siblings—Isa, Tony, and Tito—for their loyalty and support. To my sisters-in-law, Melodie and Ambar, for their words of encouragement and acts of kindness during some really difficult times.

I want to thank my sister Marizol for agreeing to share her story. For taking this huge leap of faith with me. It was a lot to ask, but I knew her story needed to be shared. Hers is a story filled with flaws and imperfections, but also honesty. It's a story that can educate and save lives, help families, friends, and communities better understand the trans experience. My sister's courage has made me a better human, and for that I am deeply grateful.

From Marizol

I remember when my sister asked me if I wanted to write a book about my experience coming out as a trans woman and all of the struggles we, trans folk, experience. Immediately, I thought, *Wow, me? Write a book? No way!* But most of my hesitation came from the simple fact that I'd never been fully open with anyone about all that I'd been through. I told her I needed some time, and after several days of reflection, I couldn't stop thinking about my trans brothers and sisters—especially those whose voices aren't usually heard. We share so many unfortunate experiences, and so few people outside of our community understand the hardships we face. This was a chance to educate others and be a source of support for so many trans folk who feel like they have none. I knew I couldn't let this opportunity to share our story pass me by. Right away, I called Seli: "Yes, Sis! I'm on board!"

To my sister, who has never given up on me, even in times when I'd given up on myself. Sis, you are one incredible woman! Where do I even begin? Thank you a million for always having my back and giving me a sense of hope. Time and time again, you've given me the will to fight, even when you were struggling to fight for yourself. Thank you for your kindness and your heart, for your generosity and advice, for your tough love.

To my parents—my king and queen—thank you for your constant, unfailing love and support. Thank you for opening your doors to me at just one month old and making me your own. I don't want to even think of what my life would have been if you hadn't taken me in. Thank you for your compassion and forgiveness and understanding, especially in the face of my past mistakes. I am forever appreciative and indebted to you. Mami and Papi, *te quiero mucho!*

To my siblings: Tony, Tito, and Isa. I know things haven't been all gravy, but no one is perfect. I want to thank you for being there and for having an open heart no matter what. To my sisters-in-law Melodie and Ambar, thank you for your love and understanding. Tony and Ambar, thank you for opening your doors to me when I needed it most. To my nieces and nephew, you are a part of why I continue to fight! You lift me up in ways you can't even imagine. Your smiles and laughs and bad jokes brighten my darkest days. You are all so appreciated and loved! And to my biological sister: I hope that this book helps you better understand a bit more of who I am. You found me two years ago and we still haven't met. I hope that we do soon, and I hope that we can build a relationship.

I am deeply grateful to the Ali Forney Center for providing me with a stable foundation, a safe space to learn and grow, and the tools to fully realize my potential. I don't know where I'd be today without your inclusive, supportive community.

From Both of Us

Many, many thanks to Laurie Smith for jumping on this ride and believing in the project from the beginning. To David R. Patterson and everyone at Stuart Krichevsky Literary Agency for their excitement for our story. To Peter Sample for his never-ending hard work and advice. To Kelli Jones and Stacey Rodriguez for their insight and enthusiasm. To the executive, editing, and production teams at Hachette Book Group and Bold Type Books who gave us this platform, especially: Katy O'Donnell for her guidance and encouragement, Kleaver Cruz for his touching handwritten note that helped us seal the deal, Beowulf Sheehan for our beautiful cover, and Pete Garceau for the artwork. To Evelyn Cruz, Marisol Solis, and Corey Tuttle for helping us look our best. To Kaitlin Carruthers-Busser, Christina Palaia, Lisa Rivlin, and everyone else involved who made our vision possible. We'd like to especially acknowledge Emily Chammah for her talent and dedication in working with us on this book. We could not have done this without her.

And finally—thank you to all of the agencies and organizations who dedicate their time to be a place of refuge, guidance, and support for the LGBTQ+ community, especially the Ali Forney Center, the Anti-Violence Project, and the Stonewall Community Foundation. And to all those brave enough to walk and live in their truth: we celebrate you.

LGBTQ+ RESOURCES FOR READERS

This list is by no means exhaustive, but we hope that readers will find the support and resources they and their loved ones need through the services provided by the organizations below. We have included local and national organizations; in many cases, the national organizations have state-by-state guides on their websites.

Community and Family Support

The Center
gaycenter.org
(212) 620-7310

The Center offers a variety of arts, entertainment, and cultural programs for LGBTQ+ individuals, in addition to serving as a community organizing space. It also offers HIV and AIDS support, individual and group counseling, health referrals, and insurance enrollment help.

The Audre Lorde Project
alp.org
(212) 463-0342 (Manhattan)
(718) 596-0342 (Brooklyn)

The Audre Lorde Project is a community center for lesbian, gay, bisexual, two-spirit, transgender, gender nonconforming, and queer people of color in New York City. It is dedicated to advocacy, coalition building, and community organizing to achieve equality and liberation.

LGBT Community Center Directory

lgbtcenters.org/lgbtcenters

CenterLink's LGBT Community Center Directory is a list of 256 LGBTQ+ community centers around the world that offer various services such as health care, counseling, and youth programs.

FIERCE

fiercenyc.org

(646) 336-6789

FIERCE is a membership-based organization in New York City open to LGBTQ+ youth of color ages thirteen to twenty-four. FIERCE members gain access to political organizing workshops, leadership development training, community events, and arts and culture programs.

PFLAG

pflag.org

(202) 467-8180

PFLAG has many chapters across the US and provides support and education for family members, friends, and allies of LGBTQ+ individuals through peer-to-peer meetings and online outreach.

TransParent

transparentusa.org

TransParent is an organization dedicated to connecting the parents of transgender and gender nonconforming children and teens. They host meetings throughout the US and equip parents with the resources needed to be as affirming, educated, and supportive as possible.

Legal Rights and Advocacy

GLAAD

glaad.org

GLAAD advocates for better depictions of LGBTQ people in media, helping to pave the way for cultural change and acceptance. Their Media Reference Guide offers tools for journalists, creators, and others who wish to portray LGBTQ people fairly and accurately.

Lambda Legal Help Desk
lambdalegal.org
(212) 809-8585 (National Headquarters)

Lambda Legal's Help Desk provides information regarding LGBTQ- or HIV-based discrimination, though it cannot offer legal advice. Those in need of assistance may call their regional office to be connected with a Help Desk representative.

Sylvia Rivera Law Project
srlp.org
(212) 337-8550

The Sylvia Rivera Law Project offers legal support (help with name changes, IDs, immigration, and more) for transgender, gender nonconforming, and/or intersex people. Under "Resources," they also provide guides to healthcare and immigration rights.

Transgender Law Center
transgenderlawcenter.org
(510) 587-9696

The Transgender Law Center offers guides to transgender individuals' rights in areas such as employment, health, immigration, policing, housing, and more.

Transgender Legal Defense & Education Fund
tldef.org/work_show.php?id=7

The Transgender Legal Defense & Education Fund's Name Change Project connects low-income transgender individuals with pro bono attorneys to assist with legal name changes.

Shelters

Ali Forney Center
aliforneycenter.org
(212) 222-3427

The Ali Forney Center provides housing, basic necessities, and supportive services (medical care, counseling, case management, and more) for homeless LGBTQ+ youth at their Drop-In Center in Manhattan.

Resources by State—The Ali Forney Center
aliforneycenter.org/get-help/resources-by-state

The Ali Forney Center hosts a list of organizations offering services to LGBTQ+ individuals outside of New York City, including shelters, community centers, and food pantries.

Casa Ruby
casaruby.org
(202) 355-5155

Casa Ruby offers housing (their free shelter is available 24-7, year-round), case management, preventative health care, and immigration services for LGBTQ+ individuals in the Washington, DC, metropolitan area.

Los Angeles LGBT Center
lalgbtcenter.org

The Los Angeles LGBT Center provides housing, health care, counseling, job training, immigration rights help, community activities, and other services for LGBTQ+ individuals in the Los Angeles area.

Health Care, Social Services, and Support

Ali Forney Center's Onsite Medical Clinic
aliforneycenter.org/programs/health-services
(212) 222-3427

The Ali Forney Center partners with the Institute for Family Health to offer HIV and HEP C testing, HIV/AIDS treatment, STI treatment, hormone replacement therapy (HRT), birth control, and other health-care services four days a week in Manhattan (see site).

Callen-Lorde Community Health Center
callen-lorde.org
(212) 271-7200

The Callen-Lorde Community Health Center offers sensitive, comprehensive health care to the New York City LGBTQ+ community regardless of one's ability to pay, including adolescent, HIV, men's, women's, transgender, mental, oral, and sexual health services.

National Center for Transgender Equality

transequality.org/know-your-rights/health-care

The National Center for Transgender Equality offers a guide to transgender health-care rights, transition-related care, and health-care enrollment, as well as "Know Your Rights" guides on subjects from airport security to employment to immigration documents and beyond.

Hetrick-Martin Institute

hmi.org
(973) 722-5060

The Hetrick-Martin Institute offers services for LGBTQ+ youth and allies (ages thirteen to twenty-four) at their locations in New York City, NY, and Newark, NJ, including counseling, case management, meals, an on-site pantry, job readiness programs, and arts and culture programs.

National Queer & Trans Therapists of Color Network

nqttcn.com

The National Queer & Trans Therapists of Color Network hosts a list of queer and transgender therapists of color around the country, as well as a list of resources for LGBTQ+ individuals.

LGBTQ+ Services—The Door

door.org/programs-services/lgbtq
(212) 941-9090 (Main)

The Door offers a wide range of services for young people in New York City, including meals, health care, legal support, counseling, job training, and LGBTQ-specific programs.

Anti-Violence Project

avp.org/get-help/get-support
(212) 714-1141

The Anti-Violence Project provides short-term counseling and legal support in the five boroughs of New York City. They also offer a 24-7, year-round crisis intervention hotline for those who are LGBTQ+, HIV-affected, and/or survivors of violence.

Suicide Prevention and Hotlines

LGBT National Help Center

glnh.org

(888) 843-4564

The LGBT National Help Center offers a free, confidential hotline from 4 p.m. to midnight EST Monday through Friday, and Saturdays from noon to 5 p.m. EST, to help LGBTQ+ individuals with coming-out issues, gender identity, relationship concerns, bullying, and more.

National Suicide Prevention Lifeline

suicidepreventionlifeline.org

(800) 273-8255

The National Suicide Prevention Lifeline offers free, confidential support to LGBTQ+ individuals, or anyone in suicidal crisis or emotional distress.

The Trevor Project

thetrevorproject.org

(866) 488-7386

If you are thinking about suicide or are feeling alone and need someone to talk to, call the Trevor Lifeline for immediate help. It's free, confidential, and available 24-7 to LGBTQ+ youth. They also offer a text-based help line that can be reached by texting START to 678678.

Trans Lifeline

translifeline.org

(877) 565-8860

The Trans Lifeline's peer-support hotline is staffed exclusively by transgender people and is available every day from 10 a.m. to 4 a.m. EST, though volunteers may be available during off-hours.

Crisis Text Line

crisistextline.org

Live, trained crisis counselors at the Crisis Text Line offer support to anyone in emotional distress. Text "HOME" to 741741 to receive 24-7 support in the US.

Sex Worker Resources

SWOP (Sex Workers Outreach Project)

swopusa.org/

The Sex Workers Outreach Project (SWOP) is a social justice network dedicated to decriminalizing sex work, advocating for sex workers' rights, and raising awareness of issues affecting sex workers. It has local chapters in many cities across the US.

DECRIMNOW

decrimnow.org/

DECRIMNOW is a Washington, DC-based movement to decriminalize sex work and advocate for the rights, health, safety, and well-being of sex workers. It hosts community and canvassing events for sex workers and their allies.

Sex Workers Project—Urban Justice Center

swp.urbanjustice.org/

(646) 602-5617

The Sex Workers Project aims to create a better world for sex workers by helping them access stable housing and safer working conditions, protect their rights in family court, clear their criminal records, secure legal immigration status, and fight police misconduct and hate crimes free of charge.

NOTES

PART II BEGINNINGS OF A TRANSITION

1. Human Rights Campaign, *Growing up LGBT in America: HRC Youth Survey Report Key Findings* (New York: Human Rights Campaign, n.d.), https://assets2.hrc.org/files/assets/resources/Growing-Up-LGBT-in-America_Report.pdf?_ga=2.150824689.618703945.1541276524-544823955.1539721769.

2. Centers for Disease Control and Prevention, *Sexual Identity, Sex of Sexual Contacts, and Health-Risk Behaviors among Students in Grades 9–12: Youth Risk Behavior Surveillance* (Atlanta, GA: US Department of Health and Human Services, 2016).

3. Jaime M. Grant, Lisa A. Mottet, Justin Tanis, with Jack Harrison, Jody L. Herman, and Mara Keisling, *Injustice at Every Turn: A Report of the National Transgender Discrimination Survey* (Washington, DC: National Center for Transgender Equality and National Gay and Lesbian Task Force, 2011), https://transequality.org/sites/default/files/docs/resources/NTDS_Report.pdf.

4. Neal A. Palmer, Emily A. Greytak, and Joseph G. Kosciw, *Educational Exclusion: Drop Out, Push Out, and the School-to-Prison Pipeline among LGBTQ Youth* (New York: GLSEN, 2016), https://www.glsen.org/research/drop-out-push-out-school-prison-pipeline.

5. Chase Strangio and Amy Fettig, "The Trump Administration Is Attacking Trans People in Federal Prison," ACLU, May 25, 2018, https://www.aclu.org/blog/lgbt-rights/criminal-justice-reform-lgbt-people/trump-administration-attacking-trans-people.

PART III   MARIZOL

1. National Center for Transgender Equality, "Know Your Rights: Social Security," https://transequality.org/know-your-rights/social-security; "Complaint Form for Allegations of Program Discrimination by the Social Security Administration" (Form SSA-437), https://www.ssa.gov/forms/ssa-437.pdf.

2. Sandy E. James, Jody L. Herman, Susan Rankin, Mara Keisling, Lisa Mottet, and Ma'ayan Anafi, *The Report of the 2015 U.S. Transgender Survey* (Washington, DC: National Center for Transgender Equality, December 2016), http://www.transequality.org/sites/default/files/docs/usts/USTS%20Full%20Report%20-%20FINAL%201.6.17.pdf.

3. "2017 Workplace Equality Fact Sheet," Out & Equal Workplace Advocates, http://outandequal.org/2017-workplace-equality-fact-sheet/.

4. National Coalition of Anti-Violence Programs (NCAVP), *Lesbian, Gay, Bisexual, Transgender, Queer, and HIV-Affected Hate Violence in 2016* (New York: Emily Waters, 2016), http://avp.org/wp-content/uploads/2017/06/NCAVP_2016HateViolence_REPORT.pdf.

5. Taylor N. T. Brown and Jody L. Herman, *Intimate Partner Violence and Sexual Abuse among LGBT People: A Review of Existing Research* (Los Angeles: Williams Institute, November 2015), https://williamsinstitute.law.ucla.edu/wp-content/uploads/Intimate-Partner-Violence-and-Sexual-Abuse-among-LGBT-People.pdf.

6. James et al., *Report of the 2015 U.S. Transgender Survey*, http://www.transequality.org/sites/default/files/docs/usts/USTS%20Full%20Report%20-%20FINAL%201.6.17.pdf.

7. National Coalition of Anti-Violence Programs (NCAVP), *Lesbian, Gay, Bisexual, Transgender, Queer, and HIV-Affected Intimate Partner Violence in 2016* (New York: Emily Waters, 2017), http://avp.org/wp-content/uploads/2017/11/NCAVP-IPV-Report-2016.pdf.

Marizol Leyva is a transgender model, cook, and activist from the Bronx. She has been featured in a cooking segment for Telemundo's *Adictivo TV* and in publications such as *Cosmopolitan*, *Latina Magazine*, *Time* magazine's Motto, and *People* magazine's Latina Love Project Series. Together with Selenis, she was awarded the Anti-Violence Project's 2016 Courage Award and the Stonewall Community Foundation's 2016 Vision Award for inspiring visibility, advocacy, and outspoken support for the transgender community.

Selenis Leyva is an award-winning American actress known for her roles as Gloria Mendoza in the Netflix hit series *Orange Is the New Black* and as Gabi Cañero in the Disney Plus original *Diary of a Future President*. In addition to her film and television credits, Selenis is an outspoken activist for LGBTQ+ rights and often is invited to college campuses to speak on diversity and inclusion. Together with Marizol, she was awarded the Anti-Violence Project's 2016 Courage Award and the Stonewall Community Foundation's 2016 Vision Award for inspiring visibility, advocacy, and outspoken support for the transgender community. She has been featured in publications such as *Splinter*, the *Huffington Post*, *Time* magazine's Motto, and *People* magazine's Latina Love Project Series. She lives in New York City.